AMERICAN GRAPHICS

RIJKSPRENTENKABINET, RIJKSMUSEUM, AMSTERDAM
May 15 through August 8, 1982

PHILADELPHIA MUSEUM OF ART
November 20, 1982, through January 16, 1983

"American Graphics" is an official project of the Netherlands-American Bicentennial Commission under the auspices of the Netherlands-American Amity Trust

The exhibition and catalogue have been made possible by a grant from the Exxon Corporation and its Netherlands' affiliate

AMERICAN GRAPHICS 1860-1940

selected from the collection of the Philadelphia Museum of Art

Introduction by Alan Fern

Catalogue by Ellen S. Jacobowitz and George H. Marcus

PHILADELPHIA MUSEUM OF ART
1982

Cover: *Brooklyn Bridge* by Louis Lozowick (no. 77)

Design by Alex Castro
Printed in the United States of America by the Meriden Gravure Company

Library of Congress Cataloging in Publication Data

Philadelphia Museum of Art.
American graphics, 1860–1940.

Exhibitions held: Rijksmuseum, Amsterdam, May 15–Aug. 8, 1982, Philadelphia Museum of Art, Nov. 20, 1982–Jan. 16, 1983.
Bibliography: p.
1. Prints, American—Exhibitions. 2. Prints—19th century—United States—Exhibitions. 3. Prints—20th century—United States—Exhibitions. I. Jacobowitz, Ellen S., 1948– II. Marcus, George H. III. Title.
NE507.P5 1982 769.973'074'014811 81-86527
ISBN 0-87633-046-4 AACR2

Contents

Preface

The United States and the Netherlands have been united in friendship for two hundred years, an anniversary that we commemorate with this exhibition, "American Graphics: 1860–1940," from the Philadelphia Museum of Art. It was to the Netherlands, especially Dutch art of the seventeenth century, that American artists first looked when over a hundred years ago they began to explore etching as a creative artistic medium. Led by the expatriate Whistler, these early participants in the American etching revival emulated Rembrandt, particularly the themes and the tonal richness of his printed works. Later, other Americans also looked to Rembrandt for inspiration: Edward Hopper, for example, for the composition of his landscapes, and Raphael Soyer, for the psychological intensity of his self-portraits and figurative works.

This exhibition also celebrates the perception and talent of Carl Zigrosser, the Museum's first Curator of Prints, who was a historian of American art and a lifelong friend of many of the artists. It was Mr. Zigrosser's activity both as curator and collector that brought to this Museum the wealth and breadth of its holdings of American graphics of this period.

We are grateful to the Netherlands-American Amity Trust and to Esso Nederland and Exxon Corporation for the support of this exhibition and catalogue. Our colleagues at the Rijksmuseum, Dr. S. H. Levie, Director General, and Dr. J. W. Niemeijer, Director of the Rijksprentenkabinet, have been most enthusiastic in welcoming this exhibition. Alan Fern, Director for Special Collections of the Library of Congress, was generous enough to provide a lively introduction to this catalogue.

JEAN SUTHERLAND BOGGS
The George D. Widener Director
Philadelphia Museum of Art

Acknowledgments

From its inception this project has had the enthusiastic support of the Netherlands-American Amity Trust, the organization that is coordinating events commemorating the two hundred years of Dutch-American friendship. They are responsible for the support generously given by Esso Nederland. We owe our thanks to those associated with the Trust, in particular, Jay Van Andel, J. Wm. Middendorf II, Charles R. Tanguy, James R. Tanis, Howard E. Daniel, Janet W. Solinger, Cynthia von Bogendorf-Rupprath, and Andries Ekker, and to Leonard Fleischer at Exxon Corporation and Ab Dercksen and Han Diepraam at Esso Nederland.

Jan Piet Filedt Kok of the Rijksmuseum cooperated in selecting the objects. With his broad knowledge he provided valuable assistance in choosing the most appropriate prints for an exhibition destined for Amsterdam. In addition, he has been a most agreeable and obliging collaborator over this past year.

At the Philadelphia Museum of Art, the following deserve thanks: Denise Thomas for her superb conservation work; Sherry Babbitt for her thorough editing and bibliographic research; Nancy Wein and Elizabeth Jarvis for their bibliographic assistance; Bernice Connolly, Dagmar Goretzki-Cofer, Sue Roberts, and Sheila Williams for their clerical efficiency; Susan Zilber and Christine Armstrong for their added support with departmental matters; Suzanne Wheeling for her preparation of the objects; and registrars Fernande Ross and Irene Taurins for their meticulous handling of the details associated with a traveling exhibition.

The following colleagues willingly gave professional advice and general support: James Bergquist, Frances Carey, Margo Dolan, Richard Field, Janet Flint, Antony Griffiths, Diane Nesley, Ann Percy, Barbara Shapiro, and Carol Troyen Lohe.

Finally it is most important to acknowledge former print curators Kneeland McNulty and the late Carl Zigrosser for their achievement in amassing the fine collection of American prints from which this exhibition is drawn, and the directors of the Philadelphia Museum of Art and the Rijksmuseum for their continued interest and encouragement.

Introduction:

The American Print

Alan Fern

Those artists who have chosen to express themselves as printmakers have given us works of unparalleled intimacy and directness. Prints are works for close and leisurely study. They bring the viewer and the creator close together, as they seem to transmit the gesture and touch of the artist with clarity and force. Prints are generally small in size, but they can be limitless in scope: they can evoke a world of shimmering beauty or stun with powerful force. Whereas paintings may stand as an artist's public voice, prints are his more private whisper.

This exhibition brings together prints from more than eight decades of American printmaking—from the collection of a single great museum print room—and includes the work of many of America's principal graphic artists. Starting with the 1850s, when Whistler emerged as the first American artist of his generation to make an impact in European art centers, and ending with the onset of the Second World War, this exhibition admirably suggests the range of artistic approaches found in America during a period of unprecedented creative activity. In the middle of the nineteenth century, when Whistler went abroad, it could fairly be said that America was a negligible force in the visual arts; after the Second World War, in contrast, New York was well on the way to replacing Paris as the center of international artistic activity. The work shown here represents what took place in those busy decades of change and chronicles the young nation's search for its genuine artistic expression.

Not all prints, however, represent an original artistic expression. Printmaking is a craft, a technique, as writing is, and like writing, may be turned to a variety of purposes. The printing of images goes back at least as far as the eighth century A.D. in China, Korea, and Japan. In fifteenth-century Europe, with the availability of paper, the multiplication of images by printing became an important force in the spread of religion, learning, and art. Since the print made possible the reproduction of a painting or a drawing, artistic productions could reach a larger audience than was previously possible. Using printmaking, maps could be replicated, books could be illustrated, views of places and portraits of people could be reproduced and published in many copies, and accurate anatomical and botanical data could be shared and transmitted. So important was this useful side of printmaking that the graphic arts were practiced in the New World very soon after the settlement of America.

Although we noted above that printmaking is a technique, it is more accurately a series of different techniques, all directed toward the same end: transferring an image from a printing surface onto a sheet of paper. These techniques vary in sophistication and complexity, and it is hardly surprising that the first prints made on this side of the Atlantic—portraits and maps—were produced with the oldest and most basic printmaking method, the woodcut. A woodcut can be made with common tools, such as knives and gouges, which are used to cut away the wood around a drawing on a block, leaving the image in relief. The wood block is then inked (as one inks a rubber stamp), a sheet of paper is placed on the inked block, and the image then transferred by rubbing or pressing the back of the paper. If the block is the same height as printing type, the relief image can be printed along with letters in a common printing press.

While relief prints were commonly used to illustrate books and newspapers, an intaglio process was more frequently employed for the production of individual prints struck from metal plates—usually copper—in the late eighteenth and early nineteenth century. This process required specialized tools (for incising metal) and printing presses, and craftsmen set up shops to serve artists and publishers in the major American cities. The example of Paul Revere—an established silversmith, yet also the publisher of several well-known prints—suggests the relationship between the metalsmith's craft and intaglio printmaking. In making a print from a metal plate, the lines to be printed are cut into the metal. The plate is then inked and the surface wiped clean, leaving ink only in the lines. The plate is covered with a sheet of dampened paper and passed through a roller press, the ink being squeezed out of the lines and imprinted on the paper under pressure. A variety of techniques can be used to incise the lines in the plate. They can be scratched or engraved directly, or etched in the metal by coating the plate with a protective varnish, scratching lines in the varnish, and placing the plate in an acid bath to etch the exposed lines.

As America became more populous and technologically advanced, a more extensive graphic arts industry arose. By the late eighteenth century, when the United States declared its independence, there were more than a few artists in America (although most still returned to England for their training), and a number of wood- and metal-engraving businesses had been established to reproduce and print their works. Maps, views, portraits, currency, political and social satires, and scientific illustrations were the stock-in-trade of the graphic craftsman in the new United States of America. The printing specialists often set up shops where both domestic and imported prints could be purchased. As in Europe, it also was possible to find prints at stationers' and booksellers' shops, and itinerant dealers served small communities and the rural public.

Specialists were even more critically needed for the production of lithographs, the system of printmaking invented at the very end of the eighteenth century by the Bavarian Aloys Senefelder. Artists found it infinitely easier to create a lithographic image than to make any other kind of print, but producing a lithograph is much more complex, requiring a press of unique design, special stones, carefully prepared and treated, and tricky presswork. Nothing has to be cut away or incised; instead, the image is drawn with a greasy crayon or ink directly on the surface of a flat block of specially prepared limestone. The stone must be chemically treated to fix the image in place, and printing is accomplished by utilizing the principle that grease and water are mutually repellent: a greasy ink rolled over the moistened stone will adhere only where the water has parted from the greasy lines of the image. In a press, a sheet of paper is forced into contact with the inked stone by a scraper, thus transferring the image. The complete process of moistening and inking is repeated for each impression printed.

By the 1820s several lithographic printers had opened establishments in the United States. By the 1840s there was a considerable lithographic industry here, and not long afterward the development of steam-driven presses made possible the production of large commercial editions. The market for prints in America was enormous. The portraits, topographic images, and genre lithographs of such publishers as Currier and Ives, Sachse, and Prang sold in the tens of thousands. Engravings of paintings by such prominent American artists as Charles Willson Peale, John Vanderlyn, and George Caleb Bingham issued by the American Art-Union and a number of other publishers made their work familiar to everyone. At the height of this activity, in the 1840s and 1850s, as many as twenty thousand copies of an engraving would have been sold, making such images as Peale's portrait of George Washington and Emanuel Leutze's *Washington Crossing the Delaware* national icons.

It is striking that most of this activity in America, at least until the 1880s, involved reproductive printmaking. Before the last quarter of the nineteenth century, few artists here seemed inclined to emulate Rembrandt or Goya by making prints as a primary creative activity. In Europe the situation was quite different. Germany, Italy, and France had an unbroken tradition of artists' printmaking. Painters frequently etched their own plates, and if they could not do the printing themselves, it was easy to locate skilled professionals to print for them. When conventional printing was too demanding or too expensive, or when an especially direct and fresh image was desired, many painters explored the monotype, taking proofs from a painting made on a sheet of metal or glass while the color was still wet, or—after the invention of photography—made *clichés-verre* by scraping an image through a varnish coating on a piece of glass and printing the plate photographically. These artists understood that direct graphic techniques were capable of expressive qualities unobtainable by any other means. They extended the artist's range as well as his audience. Working on a smaller scale and with fine lines, often in monochrome, particular aesthetic qualities came to be valued for themselves. For these artists, printmaking was anything but a reproductive process; it was instead a basic artistic medium.

The first Americans to respond to the graphic arts in this way were those who emigrated or went abroad to work for an extended period; among the earliest of these was James Abbott McNeill Whistler. In France, where he had gone to live and study, Whistler made his first etchings, and he was soon recognized as an innovator of exceptional talent and sensitivity. It surely is due as much to Whistler's concept of art as to the European environment that his work as a printmaker so quickly became important. In 1885 Whistler lectured to audiences in London, Oxford, and Cambridge about his art, stating: "Nature contains the elements, in colour and form, of all pictures, as the keyboard contains the notes of all music. . . . The artist is born to pick, and choose, and group with science, these elements, that the result may be beautiful—as the musician gathers his notes, and forms his chords, until he bring forth from chaos glorious harmony."*

In focusing upon the elements of the visual arts that were involved both in creating pictures and in eliciting a response from the viewer (in contrast to the interest in narrative, celebration of national heroes, or depiction of historical moments which had been the stock-in-trade of the "official" artist of the nineteenth century), Whistler allied himself with a new movement of independent artists. With their unconventional composition, purposeful lack of "finish," and often humble subjects, Whistler's prints (and those of his contemporaries) were of little interest to the publishers of popular engravings. His prints were sold first by painting dealers. Toward the end of the century, a few American printsellers devoted themselves to the sale of artists' prints, but the independent printmakers never enjoyed the broad public acceptance that the reproductive engravers had had earlier in the century.

Moreover, the kinds of etchings (and later, lithographs) created by artists like Whistler could not be turned over to an impersonal printer for reproduction in a large edition. The artist had either to print each proof himself or to supervise the printing of every sheet. Unless he were to spend all his time at

---

* *The Gentle Art of Making Enemies,* 2d ed., enl. (London, 1892), pp. 142–43.

the press, the artist had necessarily to limit the size of his edition. To signify his personal participation in the printing, Whistler initiated the practice of signing each proof he accepted.

A number of artists followed Whistler's example. Some, like Joseph Pennell, did so quite consciously. Others, who could not subscribe to Whistler's aesthetic position, nonetheless were inspired by his exploration of the creative possibilities of the print. Partly inspired by Whistler, but also under the influence of those who had returned from study abroad, artists in New York, Philadelphia, Cincinnati, and Baltimore established etching clubs in the 1870s and 1880s, which sponsored exhibitions and publications to make the work of their members known to the public. By the end of the century, artists in the United States had come to take the making of prints for granted.

The decades around 1900 saw the vision of American artists greatly broadened. Some, like Mary Cassatt, worked in Europe and responded to the forces that were transforming painting there. Cassatt's color prints, shaped by her close contacts with the Impressionists in Paris and by her enthusiasm for the newly discovered Japanese print, broke new ground in intaglio technique but kept to the style of representation developed by Degas, Renoir, and their colleagues. Other Americans abroad were following the work of the Nabis and other Post-Impressionists in exploring new representational modes, or were familiar with the work being done by independent artists in Italy, Germany, or Austria.

A broad selection of the new art of Europe was first shown to the American public in 1913 at the Armory Show in New York. Organized by a group led by Arthur B. Davies, whose work is included here, the Armory Show brought together artists of modernist tendencies from both sides of the Atlantic. Much of the public and most of the critics were skeptical, but the artists who saw the exhibition in New York and Chicago were unable to escape its impact. A handful of daring collectors began to acquire the works of the Cubists and their contemporaries, and the remarkable American museum collections of early twentieth-century painting had their origins at that show. Besides Davies, the Americans in this exhibition whose work was shown there included Whistler, Cassatt, George Bellows, Stuart Davis, Marsden Hartley, Childe Hassam, Edward Hopper, John Marin, Maurice Prendergast, Charles Sheeler, John Sloan, John Twachtman, and William Zorach. The Armory Show also included some of the powerful woodcuts of Edvard Munch and a substantial representation of the remarkable etchings and lithographs of Odilon Redon, who then became familiar to American artists.

Because the Armory Show took place just before the First World War, its impact was delayed. But in the 1920s, as artists resumed work, a series of new directions were defined in American printmaking. Lyonel Feininger and John Marin sought to achieve a new sense of space and form in their work in which the contours of objects were bent and shattered to communicate the energy of the city or the force of sun and wind. Marsden Hartley, Max Weber, William Zorach, and Louis Lozowick joined Feininger in this exploration of new spatial and formal representation in Europe. In their art they rejected conventional conceptions and sought to involve viewers in active emotional responses to their work, replacing the more studied and aloof evocation of beauty that underlay the work of Whistler or the comfortable sense of familiarity sought by the Impressionists.

In contrast, John Sloan and George Bellows—and later younger artists such as Grant Wood and Thomas Hart Benton—chose to celebrate American people and places using more conventional visual means. Their search for an "American" art was analogous to the literary pursuits of John Dos Passos, Sinclair Lewis, Carl Sandburg, Robert Frost, and F. Scott Fitzgerald. Like their literary counterparts, the visual artists approached their work in a variety of ways: some were impelled to comment on social conditions (especially in the big cities), some were inspired by folklore or mythology, while still others rejoiced in the beauty and diversity of the rural American landscape.

With the American scene established as a proper subject, the powerful vision of some artists transcended the ostensible theme. The clarity of form and bleakness of environment in much of Edward Hopper's work introduced an element of powerful emotion that became his trademark. Charles Sheeler's passion for the reduction of clutter and formal simplification of Shaker furniture and architecture, and the understanding of the rendition of light and shade he gained from his work as a photographer, guided him to his Precisionist paintings and lithographs of the American industrial and urban scene.

By 1930 there was a considerable spectrum of notable printmaking to be found in the United States. Even during the Great Depression, printmaking carried on. There were by then a few more galleries willing to show artists' prints, and there was a national exhibition (organized in New York by the Society of American Etchers) to which printmakers from all parts of the country could submit work. But, for all this activity, prints by American artists had no substantial market. Nonetheless, interest was kept alive.

As part of a federal relief program during the Depression, the Work Projects Administration (WPA) established printmaking workshops in many cities. At the WPA studios, artists previously unskilled in graphic techniques learned from specialists, and new techniques—notably the silk-screen print, or serigraph—were developed and popularized. Regrettably, few of the prints produced under the WPA programs merit inclusion here, but some young artists who had their first exposure to prints in this way became the teachers of the postwar generation and were instrumental in the incredible explosion of lithographic and etching printing in professional and university workshops, and in the unprecedented market for artists' prints in the 1950s and 1960s.

During the early years of the Second World War, a number of European artists came to the United States, among them the noted Surrealist printmaker Stanley William Hayter. At his Atelier 17 in Paris, Hayter had made notable advances in intaglio printmaking. He transplanted the Atelier to New York in 1940, and, surrounded by such Paris friends as Joan Miró and by many adventurous American artists, he became a central figure in the American graphic arts. He was a strong influence on such postwar masters as Mauricio Lasansky and Gabor Peterdi, who went on to set up the significant graphic workshops at the University of Iowa and the Brooklyn Museum, respectively. In Hayter's studio, such artists as Milton Avery first explored the refinements of intaglio printing. Avery's first plates had been made in the early 1930s, but editions were not pulled until he started to work with Hayter. The success of this encounter led Avery to resume making plates in the 1950s, when his work became more widely acclaimed.

Thus it was that in the 1940s American printmaking began to move from the area of private expression to a more central position in the American visual arts. The prints in this exhibition trace this journey of exploration and discovery. Although done before 1940, most of these impressions have become well known only in the past twenty-five years. One of the marks of vitality in American art life since the Second World War has been the growth of the serious study and collecting of American art. It is to be regretted that so many of the prints in this exhibition went largely unnoticed for so long. They were kept "alive" by the artists themselves, who had faith in what they had done, and by a few knowledgeable, sympathetic, and prescient scholars, curators, and dealers. Carl Zigrosser, the curator who laid the foundation of the remarkable collection of prints at the Philadelphia Museum of Art from which this exhibition is drawn, was himself a pioneering dealer in artists' prints before he joined the staff of the Museum. In his rich and long career as scholar, dealer, and curator, Zigrosser enriched our cultural life in a variety of ways. This exhibition is yet one more product of his vision and sensitivity, as we of a later generation build on what he started.

It is particularly fitting that this exhibition should come from Philadelphia, an early center of the graphic arts in America. Benjamin Franklin had his printshop there, several of the larger lithographic and commercial intaglio printshops were there in the nineteenth century, and Philadelphia was the city of Mary Cassatt, Joseph Pennell, John Sloan, and many other printmakers of exceptional talent.

Today, when all art seems to be received by a grateful and supportive public, it may be difficult for us to imagine a time when Marin's etchings or Feininger's woodcuts could not find a ready market, but such a time did exist less than half a century ago. Fortunately, artists seem to have been sustained by the curious, compelling power of prints. Whether or not they could sell, or even exhibit, their graphic works, they continued to create them. The special potential for expression that these artists realized in the etching needle, the gouge, or the lithographic crayon had an attraction that transcended the natural urge to succeed and become famous. Like drawings, many of these prints are close to the soul of the artist: they reveal his gesture, his private delights, his freshest ideas.

To study these prints is to see the panorama of American creativity in the visual arts in works that are among the most authentic, simply expressed, and deeply felt of their time. We are privileged to enjoy this carefully selected group of graphic works from one of America's great museums. It opens the door to a world of art that deserves to be better known.

CATALOGUE

James Abbott McNeill Whistler

Lowell, Massachusetts 1834–1903
London

The frequent comparisons made between Whistler and Rembrandt as etchers do not seem unjustified,* for technical virtuosity and widespread influence have given each a pivotal position in the history of printmaking. It is certainly no coincidence that Whistler's early prints bear similarities to those of his artistic predecessor, for Whistler lived at a time when etching was experiencing a revival and its leading proponents looked to Rembrandt and other Dutch artists of the seventeenth century for inspiration. Whistler acquired from Rembrandt a preference for subjects immediately at hand, focusing on city views, waterfront panoramas, and domestic interiors. Like Rembrandt, he also experimented with tonal values by varying the inking and wiping of his plates. He developed an original graphic style in which major areas of the plate were often unetched, the slight veil of ink remaining on the unetched surfaces giving his etchings a sense of softness and an evocative, atmospheric effect.

Born in Lowell, Massachusetts, Whistler spent little time in America. His father, who was commissioned by the czar to build the Moscow/Saint Petersburg railroad, moved the family to Russia in 1843. Whistler studied drawing at the Imperial Academy of Science in Saint Petersburg in 1845–46, and in 1847 he visited London on the occasion of his sister's wedding to the physician-etcher Seymour Haden, who would become a leading figure in the etching revival of the nineteenth century. After his father's death in 1849, the family returned home to America, where Whistler would remain until 1855, completing high school, attending the United States Military Academy at West Point, and working as a draftsman and cartographer.

Determined to become an artist, Whistler sailed for Europe in 1855, never to return to his native land yet never relinquishing his identity as an American. In Paris he led a bohemian life and began to paint and etch in the manner of the Barbizon artists and Courbet. Like them, he developed a strong interest in Dutch prints of the seventeenth century, especially those of Rembrandt, producing in his "French Set" (published 1858) a series of picturesque images taken directly from nature. After he moved to England in 1859, he began to etch scenes of the bustling London waterfront for what is known as the "Thames Set" (published 1871).

But the decade of the 1860s saw Whistler move away from the Realism championed by Courbet to an innovative exploration of the formal aspects of composition. For Whistler, the purpose of art was no longer the imitation of nature, but aesthetic perfection developed through a precise system of composition and color harmony, culminating in the 1870s with such masterpieces as the famous portrait of his mother. Although his work had begun to gain him recognition, a libel suit against the critic John Ruskin, albeit successful, left the artist bankrupt. To regain financial footing, he accepted a commission from a London gallery for a series of views of Venice. Whistler left for Italy in 1879, returning after more than a year in Venice with the numerous spontaneously conceived etchings later published as the first and second "Venice Sets" (in 1880 and 1886, respectively).

In the years that followed, Whistler achieved his broad international reputation. The showing of Whistler's "Mother" (Louvre, Paris) at the Pennsylvania Academy of the Fine Arts in Philadelphia in 1881 marked the beginning of his public recognition and the expansion of his artistic following in his native land.

* *See,* for example, Elizabeth Robins and Joseph Pennell, *The Life of James McNeill Whistler* (Philadelphia, 1908), vol. 1, pp. 145, 279, vol. 2, p. 125; Malcolm C. Salaman, *Modern Masters of Etching: James McNeill Whistler* (London, 1932), vol. 2, p. 3; London, Thos. Agnew & Sons Ltd., *Whistler, the Graphic Work: Amsterdam, Liverpool, London, Venice* (July 6–30, 1976), pp. 48–49; Oberlin, Ohio, Oberlin College, Allen Memorial Art Museum, *The Stamp of Whistler* (October 2–November 6, 1977), p. 4; and Claremont, Calif., Pomona College, Montgomery Art Gallery, *Whistler: Themes & Variations* (January 16–February 26, 1978), pp. 19–21.

1
The Kitchen
1858
Etching
8⅞ x 6⅛" (226 x 156 mm)
Kennedy 24 II/III
William S. Pilling Collection
43-30-13

In his choice of subject matter—a figure in a domestic interior—and his strong chiaroscuro, Whistler harks back to Rembrandt's etchings. *The Kitchen* is one of the *Douze Eaux Fortes d'après nature,* the series of twelve etchings published in 1858 and known as the "French Set." This impression is a fine example of an early *chine collé* proof pulled by the Parisian printer Auguste Delâtre on thin paper that was fused to a heavier backing sheet by the pressure of the etching press.

Whistler 1860

2
Rotherhithe

1860
Etching and drypoint
$10\frac{7}{8}$ x $7\frac{3}{4}$" (276 x 197 mm)
Kennedy 66 III/III
Purchased: Lisa Norris Elkins Fund
51-96-51

This richly inked print, etched in 1860, is from the "Thames Set," published in London in 1871 as *A Series of Sixteen Etchings of Scenes on the Thames and Other Subjects.* Here, Whistler captured the colorful dockside area of Rotherhithe below London Bridge, documenting its abundant detail with such great charm and deliberate care that this has become one of his most well-known and celebrated prints.

3
Nocturne

1878
Lithotint
$6\frac{3}{4}$ x $10\frac{1}{16}$" (171 x 259 mm)
Way 5
Staunton B. Peck Bequest
50-103-185

In this *Nocturne,* a twilight view across the Thames to the industrial area of Battersea, Whistler attempted to translate the delicate tonal gradations of his paintings of this subject into the print medium through the use of a particularly subtle lithographic technique. Printed on blue paper from a stone painted with washes of ink, this lithotint successfully captures the atmospheric qualities of Whistler's painted river views of the 1870s. Its composition, a horizontal city view seen across a watery expanse, had a great impact on Whistler's followers.

4
Old Putney Bridge

1879
Etching and drypoint
$7^{15}/_{16}$ x $11^{3}/_{4}$″ (202 x 299 mm)
Kennedy 178 IV/IV
Gift of Edward T. Ross
55-58-17

This broad view of the old wooden Putney Bridge across the Thames clearly demonstrates the influence of Japanese woodcuts on Whistler. Its subject, high horizon line, strong surface pattern, large open expanses, and juxtaposition of deep and close-up views reflect his response to the works of Hiroshige.

5
Nocturne

1879
Etching
$7^{15}/_{16}$ x $11^{9}/_{16}$" (201 x 294 mm)
Kennedy 184 IV/V
Purchased: Lisa Norris Elkins Fund
51-96-50

One of Whistler's earliest views of Venice, this etching was published in 1880 in the "First Venice Set." With its sparse etching and the veil of ink left on the plate, the poetic atmosphere of Whistler's earlier nocturnal views of the Thames is retained. Drawn directly from nature on a prepared copperplate, the image was reversed in printing: although viewed across the Gulf of Venice, the island of San Giorgio Maggiore appears on the right and the Church of the Redentore, on the left. Whistler's famous monogram, the butterfly, printed on the tab at the bottom, denoted the artist's personal acceptance of the proof.

6

The Balcony

c. 1880
Etching
$11^{11}/_{16}$ x $7^{13}/_{16}$" (296 x 198 mm)
Kennedy 207 X/XI
Gift of Bryant W. Langston
59-52-95

The complete frontality of *The Balcony,* with its abbreviated linear vocabulary focusing on central detail and its diffused atmospheric effects, was one of Whistler's most widely copied innovations. This etching is from the "Second Venice Set," published in 1886.

7

Yellow House, Lannion

1893
Color lithograph
$9^{15}/_{16}$ x $6^{7}/_{16}$" (252 x 164 mm)
Way 101
Purchased: Alice Newton Osborn Fund
1977-57-1

Unlike his several earlier color lithographs which were printed by Thomas Way in London, this view of a house in the Breton village of Lannion was pulled from five different stones by Whistler himself in his studio in Paris. Its delicate range of green, ochre, brown, gray, and black bears little resemblance to the contemporary bold and decorative lithographs designed by such artists as Toulouse-Lautrec, Bonnard, and Vuillard and printed by major French lithographic workshops.

Joseph Pennell

Philadelphia 1857–1926 Brooklyn

As Whistler's most devoted and talented American follower, Joseph Pennell became a leading figure of the American etching revival. A Philadelphian, Pennell began to study art in 1876 and was admitted to the Pennsylvania Academy of the Fine Arts in 1879. It was at the home of the president of the Academy that Pennell first saw etchings of Whistler (q.v.), Méryon, and Haden. In 1880 he withdrew from the Academy to open his own studio, supporting himself as an illustrator. He was encouraged in the field of etching by Stephen Ferris, a painter-etcher who had been one of the founders of the New York Etching Club in 1877. Through Ferris, Pennell was invited to join in the founding of the Philadelphia Society of Etchers in 1880. In 1883, Pennell first journeyed to Europe with a commission for illustrative etchings; after his marriage in 1884, he went abroad again and spent most of the next thirty-three years in Europe. Although he met Whistler in 1884, their close relationship did not commence until the 1890s.

Returning to the United States permanently in 1917, Pennell produced lithographs for the government during the war. He is remembered for his teaching and fervent lectures on wide-ranging topics at the Art Institute of Chicago and the Art Students' League in New York.

Pennell was a prolific printmaker, producing over 1,500 etchings and lithographs, mainly city views and landscapes. He followed the lead of Whistler in his passion for the etching process, his using fine papers on which to pull his proofs, his working from nature directly onto the plate, and his constant concern for tone. Pennell was an equally productive writer, known primarily for his historical and technical works on graphics, a biography of Whistler, and an autobiography.

8
Water Street Stairs, Looking Up
1881
Etching
$9\frac{7}{8}$ x $7\frac{7}{16}$" (251 x 188 mm)
Wuerth 34
Gift of Samuel L. Gerstley
55-48-24

Although executed three years before Pennell met Whistler, this striking view of Philadelphia's waterfront demonstrates that Pennell had already come under the sway of the expatriate artist through the etchings he had seen in America. The subject of a city's hidden alleyways, the rich play of light and shadow, the solid linear structure, and the spontaneity of line work are all characteristics of Whistler's early etchings.

9
From Cortlandt Street Ferry
1908
Aquatint with sandpaper ground
$12\frac{15}{16}$ x $9\frac{7}{8}$" (328 x 251 mm)
Wuerth 502
Gift of Mrs. George S.G. Cavendish, Mrs. Boyd Lee Spahr, Jr., Charles S. Wurts, and John W. Wurts
55-29-60

In an attempt to duplicate the atmospheric effects that Whistler achieved in his "Nocturnes," Pennell experimented with the use of tonal effects through aquatint and mezzotint. Echoing Whistler's views of London across the Thames, Pennell undertook this view across the river to Manhattan Island. Pennell's own success at creating a subtle, harmonious tonal composition selectively highlighted with flickering accents has made this one of his best-known images.

10

The Trains That Come and the Trains That Go

1919
Etching
$9^{15}/_{16}$ x $11^{7}/_{8}$" (253 x 302 mm)
Wuerth 712
Gift of Samuel L. Gerstley
55-48-37

Pennell's view of the Pennsylvania Railroad Station in Philadelphia, then the largest single-span train shed in the world (built 1892–93), describes its monumental scale, structural clarity, and bustling environment through an impressionistic vocabulary. Pennell praised the visual impact of the station: "Arch upon arch and tower upon tower it piles up as fine as anything abroad. . . . Philadelphians do not know that they have the most pictorial train shed in the world. . . . But there it is and when it is on a spring or fall day filled with the trains that come and that go and the smoke and steam that comes from them it is amazing, so amazing."*

* Quoted in Louis A. Wuerth, *Catalogue of the Etchings of Joseph Pennell* (Boston, 1928), p. 244, nos. 710, 712.

John Twachtman

Cincinnati 1853–1902 Gloucester, Massachusetts

John Twachtman is known primarily as a painter of atmospheric landscapes and as one of the group of American Impressionists who first exhibited in 1898 as The Ten. His graphic work is not extensive, but includes some twenty-six etchings, which in their tonal effects and sparse linearity reflect the style of Whistler (q.v.). In Cincinnati, Twachtman studied with the painter Frank Duveneck and then accompanied his teacher to Europe in 1875. Twachtman enrolled at the royal academy in Munich, a center for American art students in the 1870s, when the Munich School was emphasizing a naturalism harking back to the seventeenth century, especially to the art of Hals and Van Dyck. The next decade saw him traveling back and forth to Europe, studying in Paris, and painting on the Continent and in America. On a trip to the Low Countries in 1881, in the company of the American painter J. Alden Weir, Twachtman executed a number of etchings, often sketching on small, prepared copperplates directly from nature. Twachtman and Weir continued to share an interest in the technique of etching and in later years, when they both lived in Connecticut, they collaborated on the printing of each other's plates. By the late 1880s, Twachtman was exhibiting his paintings regularly in America and had achieved a measure of popularity and success. In 1889 he joined the faculty of the Art Students' League in New York, and in 1894 he began to teach at the Cooper Union in the same city.

11

Boats on the Maas

1881–83
Etching
12 7/16 x 17 3/4″ (316 x 450 mm) (image)
Anonymous gift
52-80-12

In this large etching of boats on the river Meuse (Maas), the horizon line and emphasis on midground elements recall Rembrandt's landscapes, but the economy of the richly inked lines and the handling of the watery expanse reveal the influence of Whistler. By leaving a slight veil of brown ink on the plate, Twachtman supplied an overall tone for the landscape, which he surrounded with an etched line. The choice of shiny vellum paper intensified the brilliance and shimmering effect of the scene.

Mary Cassatt

Allegheny City, Pennsylvania
1845–1926 Mesnil-Theribus (Oise)

In the more than two hundred prints that she executed between 1879 and 1911, Mary Cassatt portrayed the genteel domesticity of the life she enjoyed as an expatriate in Paris. Her interest in art probably developed during the early years she spent abroad with her family, and she seriously began to pursue artistic studies at the age of sixteen, when she enrolled at the Pennsylvania Academy of the Fine Arts in Philadelphia. In 1866 she left for Europe, where she would remain for virtually the rest of her life. After studying in France, then Parma, and traveling extensively, she settled in Paris in 1874. In 1872 she had already sent a painting to the Paris Salon, and she continued to exhibit there until 1876, although she was often dissatisfied with the jury and Salon standards. Degas was taken with her work when he saw it at the Salon, and in 1877 he invited her to exhibit with the group of artists who would become known as the Impressionists; she was the only American to be part of this group. It is their influence that appears most strongly in Cassatt's graphic work, and it was through their encouragement, especially that of Degas, that she devoted a great deal of time to experimenting with various graphic techniques. In her later years, Cassatt's activity slowed as her eyesight began to fail; she finally stopped work on her drypoints in 1911 and on her paintings in 1914.

When Americans traveled abroad in the 1890s and early 1900s, they often called on Mary Cassatt, who applied great energy to advising them on the acquisition of paintings for their collections. Her impact is mirrored in the marvelous examples of Impressionist painting now in American museums, many of which were first purchased privately on her advice.

12
In the Opera Box
c. 1880
Soft-ground etching and aquatint
8³⁄₁₆ x 7½" (208 x 190 mm)
Breeskin 22 III/III
Acquired by exchange
61-191-14

This charming image of a young woman at the opera was one of a number of prints intended for a journal entitled "La Jour et la Nuit," which Degas began planning in 1879 but never published. The use of soft-ground etching combined with aquatint and burnishing allowed Cassatt to achieve an effect of tone and color recalling Degas's monotypes.

13
Lady in Black, in a Loge, Facing Right

c. 1881
Soft-ground etching and aquatint
7⅝ x 11$\frac{9}{16}$″ (193 x 293 mm)
Breeskin 24 III/III
Gift of Mrs. Horace Binney Hare
56-113-1

In scenes such as this candid view of a woman in her loge at the opera, Cassatt followed the attraction that the theater had for the Impressionist painters, especially Degas and Manet.

14
Tea

1890
Drypoint
$7\frac{3}{16}$ x $6\frac{3}{16}$" (182 x 157 mm)
Breeskin 133 V/V
William S. Pilling Collection
40-8-1

Degas encouraged Cassatt to refine her drawing skills, and he may indeed have urged her to work directly on the copperplate. The drypoint technique most challenged her graphic precision while the burr of the copper gave a soft edge to her line. Like Whistler (q.v.), Cassatt left a slight veil of ink on the plate and chose an antique laid paper to add tonal qualities to her composition.

15
The Letter

1891
Color print with drypoint and aquatint
$13\frac{9}{16}$ x $8\frac{7}{8}$" (345 x 226 mm)
Breeskin 146 III/III
The Louis E. Stern Collection
63-181-122

Inspired by her visit to a large exhibition of Japanese prints in Paris in 1890, Cassatt produced a series of ten brilliant color prints. That summer she set up an etching press and employed a professional printer to assist her with the laborious task of pulling the proofs. By carefully planning the distribution of her colors, a number of which were applied to the same plate, she was able to print each of her subjects from no more than three copperplates and to keep the colors distinct. The Japanese influence is evident in the diagonal perspective, rich overall patterns, emphasis on distinct flat areas of color, high viewpoint, and asymmetry of the composition.

16

Sara Wearing Her Bonnet and Coat

c. 1904
Lithograph
19 13/16 x 16 3/8" (504 x 416 mm)
Breeskin 198
Purchased: Thomas Skelton Harrison Fund
60-56-1

This unusually large composition, one of only two lithographs produced by Cassatt, was freely drawn on paper with a crayon and transferred to the stone for printing. It has been suggested that the model was the granddaughter of Émile Loubet,* who was president of France from 1899 to 1906. Cassatt may have met Loubet through her friendship with Georges Clemenceau.

* Adelyn Dohme Breeskin, *Mary Cassatt: A Catalogue Raisonné of the Oils, Pastels, Watercolors, and Drawings* (Washington, D.C., 1970), p. 150, no. 351.

John Singer Sargent

Florence 1856–1925 London

As one of the leading portraitists of his day, John Singer Sargent was constantly in demand by a fashionable clientele on both sides of the Atlantic, and he traveled extensively throughout his much-celebrated career. Born to an American family living in Florence, Sargent did not visit the United States until 1876. He was educated on the Continent, and in 1874 he entered the atelier of the French painter Carolus-Duran. Both the admiration for Velázquez fostered in his master's studio and his own fascination with Frans Hals combined to form the elements of Sargent's brilliant style—bravura draftsmanship, spontaneity of execution, and preoccupation with light—tempered by the influence of the Impressionists and Whistler (q.v.).

Sargent was primarily a painter, not a printmaker, and only six lithographs by him are known. His first two lithographs were executed in 1895 at the invitation of the artists Lord Frederick Leighton and Alfred Gilbert, who were organizing the British contribution to a Paris exhibition celebrating the centennial of lithography.* The printer Frederick Goulding supplied Sargent, Leighton, Alma-Tadema, and a number of other distinguished artists with crayons and transfer paper, the drawings then being transferred to stones for printing by Goulding's firm. After the exhibition in Paris, the lithographs were shown at the Rembrandt Gallery in London in November 1895.

* Martin Harding, *Frederick Goulding: Master Printer of Copper Plates* (Stirling, Scotland, 1910), pp. 106–11.

17
Study of a Draped Nude
1895
Lithograph
11⅝ x 8⅝" (296 x 219 mm)
Purchased: Thomas Skelton Harrison Fund
41-53-57

Drawn in the spirited style of Sargent's crayon studies, this is one of the two works by Sargent printed for the 1895 exhibition of lithographs by well-known artists.

William Merritt Chase

Williamsburg, Indiana 1849–1916
New York

After studying at the royal academy in Munich from 1872 to 1877 and spending the year 1877–78 in Venice, William Merritt Chase returned to the United States to become one of the leading figures in American art education. He revolutionized the character of American art as a teacher of private students in the European tradition, most notably at his Tenth Street Studio, and as an instructor at the Art Students' League in New York for twenty-one years, at the Chase School (renamed the New York School of Art), which he founded in 1896, for twelve years, and at the Pennsylvania Academy of the Fine Arts in Philadelphia for thirteen years. His early students followed his use of a somber palette and his spontaneous, rich application of paint, based on the style of the Munich School. Later, in the 1880s and 1890s, he developed a more modern, brilliant plein air style influenced by Impressionism, which then became the basis of his teaching. The summer school that Chase held at Shinnecock Hills on eastern Long Island from 1891 to 1902, when his own finest landscapes were done, was especially influential. He served as president of the Society of American Artists in 1880 and again from 1885 to 1895. He was, however, sympathetic to the artists who resigned from that organization to exhibit in 1898 as The Ten, and in 1902 was himself elected to the group.

While Chase produced several etchings, the freer monotype process was more compatible with his rapid painting style. He may have learned this technique in 1877–78 in Venice, where he had gone with John Twachtman (q.v.) and Frank Duveneck (with whom he had shared a studio in Munich). Monotypes were being made in Venice "as means of entertainment" by American and English artists, led by Otto Bacher, an American student of Duveneck.* Chase first exhibited his monotypes soon after his return to New York in 1878.

* David Kiehl, "American Monotypes," in Boston, Museum of Fine Arts, *Art & Commerce* (Charlottesville, Va., 1978), pp. 153–54.

18
Portrait of a Man
c. 1890
Monotype
7¾ x 5¹⁵⁄16″ (197 x 150 mm)
Purchased: Marie Josephine Rozet Fund
75-162-1

Because of Chase's position as artist and teacher, he played a key role in popularizing the monotype process in America. This technique allowed him to paint with his brush directly on a plate from which one or a few proofs could be printed before the ink or paint dried. Most of his known monotypes are portraits, and like this one, done in a single color.

Maurice Prendergast

Saint John's, Newfoundland
1859–1924 New York

Prendergast lived most of his life in Boston and nearby Winchester. His first thirty years are poorly documented, but it is known that he supported himself as a calligrapher and taught himself the fundamentals of sketching and painting. Studying in Paris from 1891 to 1895, he enrolled at the Académie Julian and the Académie Colarossi. During this and a subsequent trip to Europe in 1898–99, Prendergast began to develop an original style of painting in broad areas of color with strong, rapid brushstrokes that was influenced chiefly by the Post-Impressionists and the Nabi painters Vuillard and Bonnard. In the some two hundred monotypes that he made from about 1891 to 1902 he found a ready vehicle for the quickness of execution he favored in his painting. In a letter of 1905, Prendergast outlined his monotype method: "Paint on copper in oils, wiping parts to be white. When picture suits you, place on it Japanese paper and either press in a press or rub with a spoon till it pleases you. Sometimes the second or third plate [proof] is the best."*

From the time of his return from Paris in 1895, he began to exhibit regularly, gaining a wide following in America. In 1908 he exhibited at the Macbeth Gallery in New York as a member of The Eight, although his work did not include the social concerns of many in that group. He was included in the Armory Show of 1913, and the following year he moved to New York.

* Quoted in Hedley Howell Rhys, *Maurice Prendergast* 1859–1924 (Cambridge, Mass., 1960), p. 34.

19
The Breezey Common
c. 1895–97
Color monotype
6½ x 5" (165 x 128 mm)
Gift of the Friends of the Philadelphia Museum of Art
64-205-3

Reminiscent of the vignettes of Bonnard and Vuillard, this color monotype shows two women and a child strolling on a grassy expanse in the Boston Common as schoolgirls gambol beyond. This is one of three related monotypes bearing the same title (private collections).

John Sloan

Lock Haven, Pennsylvania 1871–1951 Hanover, New Hampshire

From 1891 to 1903 John Sloan supported himself as an illustrator, working for the *Philadelphia Inquirer* and the *Philadelphia Press.* He had little formal artistic training although he did take several classes in drawing, notably one with Thomas Anshutz at the Pennsylvania Academy of the Fine Arts in Philadelphia in 1892–93. Most significant, however, was his friendship with the painter Robert Henri, a teacher at the Academy, under whose encouragement he began to paint in 1897. In 1904, again with the encouragement of Henri and others of his coterie, Sloan moved to New York, where in 1908 he exhibited with the group called The Eight. Lead by Henri, these artists—Sloan, William Glackens, George Luks, Everett Shinn, Arthur B. Davies (q.v.), Maurice Prendergast (q.v.), and Ernest Lawson—sought alternatives to the art of the Academy. Sloan served as art editor of the Socialist magazine *The Masses* from 1912 to 1916. He also taught for twenty-two years at the Art Students' League, where his students included Reginald Marsh, Raphael Soyer (qq.v.), and Alexander Calder. His lectures were recorded in 1939 by his student (later his wife) Helen Farr in *Gist of Art.*

Sloan taught himself to etch by studying *The Etcher's Handbook* of Philip Gilbert Hamerton (3rd ed., London, 1881). He made some fifty etchings for a publisher of calendars and novelties before his first important commission in this medium came in 1902, when he was asked to illustrate a deluxe edition of novels by the French writer Charles Paul de Kock, for which Sloan produced fifty-three etchings. In 1905–6, he made ten etchings for his "New York City Life" series, and he continued to use the city as the inspiration for his social and satirical themes.

Sloan was dedicated to the process of etching as an art form. He repeatedly worked his themes through on the plate—often even after having made full preparatory studies on transfer tissue—frequently etching a separate state for as few as one or two changed lines; some of his prints are known in as many as ten states, and one, in twenty-nine.

The Philadelphia Museum of Art houses the most important collection of Sloan's graphic work, including more than nine hundred preparatory drawings, early states, proof states, and published prints, acquired from the artist's widow.

20

Turning Out the Light

1905
Etching
$4^{13}/_{16}$ x $6^{7}/_{8}$″ (122 x 174 mm)
Morse 134 III/III
Gift of Mrs. Alice Newton Osborn
59-35-59

Turning Out the Light is one of the ten etchings from Sloan's "New York City Life" series. A subject such as this, showing a couple in bed, was quite daring in America, and four prints from the series were rejected as "vulgar" and "indecent" when they were submitted to the exhibition of the American Water Color Society in 1906.

21

Copyist at the Metropolitan Museum

1908
Etching
$7^{3}/_{16}$ x $8^{3}/_{4}$″ (183 x 222 mm)
Morse 148 VIII/VIII
Purchased: Lola Downin Peck Fund from the Carl and Laura Zigrosser Collection
67-31-69

Sloan had little respect for those who copied art rather than life on their canvases. In his diary, he recorded that he went to the Metropolitan Museum of Art "where the 'Copyists' at work are very amusing" and, later, that he "started to make a plate of a copyist at work in the Metropolitan Museum of Art, crowd around as it is a sheep picture which the lay copyist is 'takin' off'."* Sloan portrayed himself and his wife Dolly as the two visitors in the left foreground.

* Quoted in Bruce St. John, ed., *John Sloan's New York Scene* (New York, 1965), pp. 130, 244.

22

Anshutz on Anatomy

1912
Etching
$7^{5}/_{16}$ x $8^{7}/_{8}$" (186 x 225 mm)
Morse 155 VIII/VIII
Purchased: Lessing J. Rosenwald gift and Katharine Levin Farrell Fund income
56-35-83

Thomas Anshutz succeeded Thomas Eakins as the head of the life class at the Pennsylvania Academy of the Fine Arts, continuing to follow Eakins's intensive routine of instruction in anatomy. Sloan studied with Anshutz at the Academy, and in 1912 he made this etching of a lecture Anshutz had given some years earlier to Robert Henri's students at the New York School of Art. Anshutz is shown holding a ball of clay which he would use to form muscles on the skeleton, the human model nearby then being asked to demonstrate muscular activity. Sloan drew a number of his friends among the observers, including Henri, Prendergast, and George Bellows (q.v.), and portrayed himself as the figure with eyeglasses at the upper right.

23
Arch Conspirators

1917
Etching
4⅛ x 5 13/16" (105 x 148 mm)
Morse 183 II/II
Purchased: Lessing J. Rosenwald gift and Katharine Levin Farrell Fund income
56-35-110

In one of but a few instances of youthful bohemianism, Sloan joined several other residents of New York's Greenwich Village on a cold night in January 1917, when they stole up to the top of Washington Arch at the foot of Fifth Avenue for a midwinter party. In the course of the evening these "Arch Conspirators" drew up a document calling for the secession of Greenwich Village from the United States. Among the participants, Marcel Duchamp is shown standing at the left and Sloan, crouching at the right.

24
Hell Hole

1917
Etching and aquatint
$7\frac{7}{8}$ x $9\frac{3}{4}$" (200 x 248 mm)
Morse 186 II/II
Purchased: Lessing J. Rosenwald gift and Katharine Levin Farrell Fund income
56-35-109

Here Sloan pictures a gathering place for artists and writers that he frequented at Sixth Avenue and West Fourth Street in Greenwich Village, nicknamed the "Hell Hole." The playwright Eugene O'Neill is the figure at the upper right.

25

Sunbathers on the Roof

1941
Etching
$5^{7}/_{8}$ x $6^{15}/_{16}$" (149 x 176 mm)
Morse 307
Purchased: Lessing J. Rosenwald gift and Katharine Levin Farrell Fund income
56-35-219

In a statement that accompanied this etching when it was sent to members of the American College Society of Print Collectors, Sloan described the rooftop life of New York that fascinated him so much: "In the spring as the rays grow warmer, the tenement roofs in New York begin to come to life. More washes are hung out—gay colored underthings flap in the breezes, and on Saturdays and Sundays girls and men in bathing togs stretch themselves on newspapers, blankets or sheets in the sun, turning over at intervals like hotcakes. I think that many of them are acquiring a coat of tan in preparation for coming trips to Coney Island. The roof life of the Metropolis is so interesting to me that I am almost reluctant to leave in June for my summer in Santa Fe."*

* Quoted in Peter Morse, *John Sloan's Prints* (New Haven, 1969), no. 307.

26

Snowstorm in the Village

1925
Etching
$6\frac{15}{16}$ x 5″ (176 x 126 mm)
Morse 216 III/III
Purchased: Lessing J. Rosenwald gift and Katharine Levin Farrell Fund income
56-35-131a

This wonderful depiction of the Sixth Avenue elevated train tracks in Greenwich Village as seen from his studio during a snowstorm is Sloan's most impressionistic etching.

Childe Hassam

Dorchester, Massachusetts 1859–1935
Easthampton, New York

Childe Hassam began his career in Boston as a magazine and book illustrator. He studied painting at the Boston Art Club, and in 1883 he took his first trip abroad. Two years later he returned to Paris, where he followed the course of study at the Académie Julian, producing works in the traditional style of the Salon that won him a bronze medal at the Paris Exposition of 1889. He also saw the art of Monet and other Impressionists and began to introduce their concern for color and light into his painting. He may also have met the Nabi painters at the Académie Julian, for elements of their style may be found in his later work. Hassam returned to America in 1889 and settled in New York. Over the next years he evolved his own impressionistic style of plein air landscape painting for which he became well known. He was one of the group of painters who in 1898 broke away from the Society of American Artists and exhibited as The Ten.

It was not until 1915 that Hassam seriously took up etching. That year he made some 60 etchings, many drawn in the quaint village of Cos Cob in southern Connecticut, successfully translating into etched lines the atmospheric and tonal concerns of his paintings. He continued to etch into the 1930s, and his total *oeuvre* includes over 350 etchings and drypoints. Hassam was a pioneer in the revival of the artistic use of lithography in America, producing some 45 lithographs during 1917 and 1918, which were not, however, a commercial success.

27
Old Lace

1915
Etching
6⅞ x 6⅞" (175 x 175 mm)
Cortissoz 56
Gift of Mrs. Childe Hassam
40-21-46

Like the Impressionists, particularly Monet and Pissarro, Hassam worked directly from nature in this view of an inlet along the Connecticut shore at Cos Cob. Its delicate etching produced a soft allover pattern that suggested to the artist the title *Old Lace.*

28

Dutch Door

1915
Etching
8¼ x 9 13/16″ (210 x 249 mm)
Cortissoz 49
Gift of Mrs. Childe Hassam
40-21-47

This scene of a woman at a door, executed in 1915 in Cos Cob, recalls the intimate, light-filled interiors of Bonnard and Vuillard, whose work influenced Hassam.

29
Washington's Birthday—Fifth Avenue and 23rd Street

1916
Etching
12 13/16 x 7" (326 x 178 mm)
Cortissoz 68 II/II
Gift of Bryant W. Langston
58-149-31

During World War I, Hassam did a series of patriotic paintings of New York's Fifth Avenue hung with the flags of the Allies, reminiscent of the boulevard scenes of Pissarro. Related to his "Flag" series, this etching shows a crowded Fifth Avenue, with the famed Flatiron Building in the distance.

30
French Cruiser

1918
Lithotint
8 13/16 x 12 15/16″ (224 x 328 mm)
Griffith 13
Gift of Mrs. Childe Hassam
40-21-20

In its composition, subject, and tonal harmony, Hassam's simple, bold lithotint shows the lasting influence of Whistler on American art.

31

The Lion Gardiner House, Easthampton

1920
Etching
9¾ x 14⅛″ (248 x 359 mm)
Cortissoz 159
Gift of Bryant W. Langston
58-149-32

A number of Hassam's richest etchings were done in Easthampton, one of the oldest towns on eastern Long Island, where he spent many summers. Here his concern for color, light, and shadow is beautifully conveyed in one of Hassam's best-known prints.

George Bellows

Columbus, Ohio 1882–1925 New York

George Bellows was one of America's most successful and popular painters and printmakers. With his vigorous style and his themes taken from the life around him, he created a truly American idiom. Born in Columbus, Ohio, Bellows went to New York in 1904 and studied at the New York School of Art with William Merritt Chase (q.v.) and Robert Henri. Quickly he made a name for himself and within five years became the youngest Associate elected to the National Academy of Design. From 1910 to 1911 and 1917 to 1919, he taught at the Art Students' League, and from 1912 to 1917 he was a staff member and illustrator for the radical magazine *The Masses.* He exhibited five paintings and four drawings at the Armory Show in 1913.

In 1916 Bellows first became interested in the methods of lithography, a medium then seldom exploited for artistic purposes because of its associations with commercial printing. "I have been doing what I can," he wrote in 1917, "to rehabilitate the medium from the stigma of commercialism which has attached to it so strongly. I didn't have this motive as a starter and it is by no means dominant. . . . The mechanics are such as to drive away the artists who contemplate its use."* Before this era, the laborious task of printing lithographs and the lack of ateliers for artistic purposes had discouraged artists in America from using lithographic techniques. Most of Bellows's own stones were printed in the lithographic shops of George Miller (from 1916 to 1919) and Bolton Brown (from 1921 to 1924). The 193 images and nearly 8,000 impressions made by the time of his death at the age of forty-two could not have been accomplished without their collaboration.

* Bellows to Joseph Taylor, March 15, 1917, quoted in Chicago, The Art Institute of Chicago, *George Bellows: Paintings, Drawings and Prints* (January 31–March 10, 1946), p. 33.

32
Benediction in Georgia

1916
Lithograph
16¼ x 20⅛" (413 x 511 mm)
Beer 135, Mason 12
Gift of the American Federation of Arts
43-79-4

Many of Bellows's finest lithographs are incisive satires on the religious and political life of America. This composition of a Southern white minister preaching to black convicts was published in the May 1917 issue of *The Masses,* a left-wing magazine published between 1911 and 1917.

33

Dance in a Madhouse

1917
Lithograph
18¼ x 24$^{5}/_{16}$" (464 x 618 mm)
Beer 92, Mason 49
SmithKline Corporation Collection
58-150-8

Here Bellows drew on early memories of a mental hospital he visited when, as he described, he was "an intimate friend of the family of the superintendent of the great State Hospital at Columbus, Ohio. For years the amusement hall was a gloomy old brown vault where on Thursday nights the patients indulged in 'Round Dances' interspersed with two-steps and waltzes by the visitors. Each of the characters in this print represents a definite individual. Happy Jack boasted of being able to crack hickory nuts with his gums. Joe Peachmyer was a constant borrower of a nickel or a chew. The gentleman in the center had succeeded with a number of perpetual motion machines. The lady in the middle center assured the artist by looking at his palm that he was a direct descendant of Christ. This is the happier side of a vast world which a more considerate and wiser society could reduce to a not inconsiderable degree."*

* Quoted in Lauris Mason and Joan Ludman, *The Lithographs of George Bellows* (Millwood, N.Y., 1977), p. 92.

34
A Stag at Sharkey's

1917
Lithograph
18¾ x 23$^{11}/_{16}$" (476 x 602 mm)
Beer 71, Mason 46
Gift of Mr. and Mrs. George Sharp Munson
51-9-1

Bellows is known widely for his prizefight scenes, and *A Stag at Sharkey's* is one of the most famous images of American art. Prizefighting was outlawed as a public event in New York City, and thus bouts were held in the back rooms of saloons such as Sharkey's Club, where this fight took place. This lithograph is based on a painting done in 1907, now in the Cleveland Museum of Art.

35
River-Front

1923–24
Lithograph
$14^{15}/_{16}$ x $20^{15}/_{16}$″ (380 x 532 mm)
Beer 24, Mason 168
Gift of Dr. F. H. Hirschland
51-67-9

In many of Bellows's later works, such as this lithograph of a crowd of youths sunbathing and swimming in New York's East River, the artist was as concerned with the geometry of his compositions as with the individualization of his figures.

36
Sixteen East Gay Street

1923–24
Lithograph
9½ x 11⅞″ (241 x 302 mm)
Beer 84, Mason 183
Purchased: Staunton B. Peck Fund
65-95-49

Hometown, America! A visit back home probably inspired this view of Columbus, Ohio, which captures the timeless quality of life in a Midwestern town.

GEO BELLOWS
Bolton Brown. imp.
Jean in a Black Hat
Geo Bellows

37
Jean in a Black Hat

1923–24
Lithograph
10 11/16 x 9 1/8" (272 x 232 mm)
Beer 126, Mason 187 II/II
Gift of Bryant W. Langston
59-52-4

Bellows executed many lithographs of his family, including this study of his daughter Jean at the age of eight or nine. The black hat was a motif that Bellows used in portraits of various sitters.

38
Nude Study (Girl Standing on One Foot)

1923–24
Lithograph
12 1/4 x 5" (311 x 127 mm)
Beer 148, Mason 175
Purchased: Staunton B. Peck Fund
65-95-46

This is one of a series of eight lithographs devoted to the subject of the female nude that Bellows did the year before he died.

B. J. O. Nordfeldt

Tullstorp (Skåne), Sweden 1878–1955
Henderson, Texas

Although B.J.O. Nordfeldt's modernist paintings were not well received by critics when they were exhibited in America in the first decades of this century, his etchings, executed in a style derived from Whistler, and his color woodcuts were repeatedly praised. Born in Sweden, Nordfeldt came to America with his family in 1891, settling in Chicago. While enrolled at the Art Institute of Chicago in 1899, he was chosen to assist with a large mural being painted for the McCormick Harvester Company and was sent to Paris to supervise its installation at the Exposition of 1900. He remained abroad until 1903, first painting in Paris, then studying the technique of Japanese wood-block printing in England with Frank Morley Fletcher, the well-known graphic artist who had introduced this process into Britain. After his return to Chicago, Nordfeldt became one of the pioneers of the woodcut revival in America. Over the next years he traveled widely in Europe and America, fulfilling commissions for magazine illustrations and etchings. In 1914 he moved to New York and began to spend his summers in Provincetown on the tip of Cape Cod, Massachusetts. He was one of the founders of the Provincetown Players, designing sets and acting with this theater group noted for its early productions of plays by Eugene O'Neill. He was also one of the organizers of the Provincetown Printers, the first society in America devoted solely to wood-block printing, which made Provincetown a center for experimentation with this medium. In 1919 Nordfeldt moved West, painting Indian subjects in Santa Fe which are among his best-known works. In 1937 he returned East, establishing a studio in Lambertville, New Jersey.

39
The Long Wave
c. 1906
Color woodcut
$7\frac{5}{8}$ x $14\frac{15}{16}$" (194 x 379 mm)
Gift of Mrs. B.J.O. Nordfeldt
57-46-4

Nordfeldt's debt to Frank Morley Fletcher and Japanese wood-block prints is demonstrated by the subject of *The Long Wave*—a reference to famous prints of waves by Hokusai and Hiroshige—and by its drawn border and refined, careful execution.

40

Rocks by Shore

1906
Color woodcut
8¼ x 13¹¹⁄₁₆″ (210 x 347 mm)
Gift of Mrs. B.J.O. Nordfeldt
57-46-5

The flat areas of color and the subtle harmonies of the rocks and sea are derived from Fletcher's interpretation of Japanese prints.

William Zorach

Eurburg, Lithuania 1889*–1966 Bath, Maine

Known primarily as a sculptor, William Zorach began his career as a painter and printmaker. Emigrating from Lithuania, his family settled in Cleveland, where he attended night classes at the Cleveland School of Art and worked by day for a commercial lithographer. To further his art education he moved to New York in 1908, enrolling at the National Academy of Design. In 1910 he went to Paris, where he studied painting and worked in an Impressionist style. The paintings of the Fauves and Post-Impressionists that he saw in Europe would not affect his own paintings until around 1912, when his lack of success on his return to America—or the impact of the Fauve paintings of his new wife Marguerite, whom he had met in Paris—perhaps prompted an abrupt change in his work. Two canvases done in his new style were accepted by the jury for the American section of the Armory Show in 1913. His expressive use of abstract, flat areas of bright color and later his Cubist-inspired style made him one of the earliest modernist artists working in America.

Zorach first experimented with color wood-block printing during the summer of 1916 in Provincetown, Massachusetts. He joined B.J.O. Nordfeldt (q.v.) and others in the first American wood-block print society, the Provincetown Printers, and participated in exhibitions of this group. In 1917, while working on wood blocks, he made his first wood carving, and soon he began to concentrate on sculpture, abandoning oil painting in 1922.

* The traditional birthdate of 1887 has been disputed by recent research. *See* Roberta Kupfrian Tarbell, "Catalogue Raisonné of William Zorach's Carved Sculpture" (Ph.D. diss., University of Delaware, 1976), vol. 1, p. 5n.

41
Head of a Girl

c. 1917
Color stencil print
9¾ x 4¼" (248 x 108 mm)
Anonymous gift
49-76-9

Previously considered one of Zorach's relief-printed works, the Cubist *Head of a Girl* recently has been identified as a four-color stencil print,* an example of the artist's experimentation with various print mediums.

* This information was obtained through communication with Janet A. Flint, Curator of Prints and Drawings, National Museum of American Art, Smithsonian Institution, Washington, D.C.

42
Ship and Swimming Figures

c. 1915–17
Color relief print
6⁵⁄₁₆ x 7⁹⁄₁₆" (160 x 192 mm)
Purchased: Lola Downin Peck Fund from the Carl and Laura Zigrosser Collection
74-24-250

This playful composition of two figures swimming, with a three-masted ship beyond, exemplifies the artist's decorative and simplified style. The ship and waves are printed in flat areas of dark colors, leaving the white of the paper to give form to figures and birds and to define the linear details.

Max Weber

Bialystok, Russia 1881–1961 Great Neck, New York

Max Weber was one of the earliest American modernist artists to experiment with color relief printing, finding this medium well suited to his expressionistic style. When Weber was ten, his family came to America and settled in Brooklyn. His art education began there in 1898 with three years at the Pratt Institute of Art, where he studied with the painter Arthur Wesley Dow, who drew on the color theory of Gauguin (whom Dow had encountered in Pont Aven in 1886) and the flat patterns of Japanese prints to emphasize overall design rather than naturalism. In 1905 Weber journeyed to Paris, studying painting and traveling for long periods in Spain, Italy, and the Low Countries. On his return to New York in 1909 he met Alfred Stieglitz; two years later his one-man exhibition at Stieglitz's "291" gallery provoked violent attacks from the critics. Even in the face of this disparaging criticism and lack of success, Weber continued to paint in a personal style derived from the works of Cézanne, Matisse (with whom he studied), Henri Rousseau, and Picasso and influenced by the expressiveness of so-called primitive art. He supported himself by teaching at the White School of Photography (1914–18) and at the Art Students' League (1920–21 and 1925–27). Recognition and patronage began to come only after the mid-1920s, culminating in a retrospective exhibition in 1930 at the newly formed Museum of Modern Art in New York.

Weber's graphic work includes some forty-five woodcuts and linoleum cuts, most executed in 1919 and 1920; his friendship with Zorach (q.v.) and the New York exhibitions of the Provincetown Printers perhaps inspired his relief-printing activity. His wood-block prints are notable for their color harmonies and the uniqueness of each impression. Following the color-printing innovations of Nordfeldt (q.v.) at this time, he often used only one block for each image, printing up to ten colors at once from the block. In other instances, he printed a single, or several blocks successively, one color at a time. Weber also executed some sixty lithographs between 1916 and 1932.

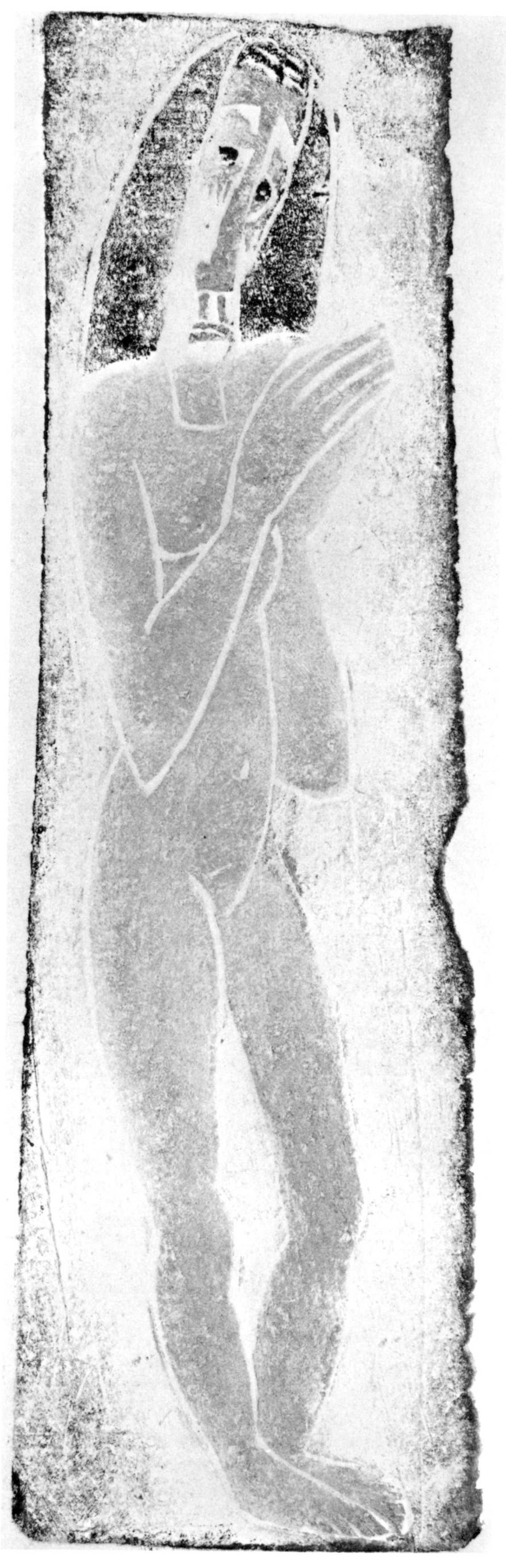

43
Prayer

1920
Color linoleum cut
9 x $2\frac{13}{16}$" (229 x 71 mm)
Rubenstein 32
Purchased: Thomas Skelton Harrison Fund
42-30-102

According to Rubenstein, the praying figure in this linoleum cut has prototypes in the Tahitian nudes of Gauguin.*

* Daryl R. Rubenstein, *Max Weber: A Catalogue Raisonné of His Graphic Work* (Chicago, 1980), p. 46.

44
Mother Love (Madonna and Child)

1919–20
Color woodcut
$7\frac{3}{4}$ x $2\frac{1}{16}$" (196 x 53 mm)
Rubenstein 35
Purchased: Staunton B. Peck Fund
65-95-481

The Yiddish phrase for "mother love" is inscribed under this group of a mother and child, an image related to Byzantine icons of madonnas that Weber had seen in his native Russia. The forms are defined by reserved lines—the incised areas of the block that did not hold ink—a technique not unlike that also used by William Zorach (*see* no. 42).

45
Invocation

1919–20
Color woodcut
3¾ x 2³⁄₁₆″ (95 x 55 mm)
Rubenstein 27
Purchased: Staunton B. Peck Fund
65-95-478

The spirituality and forms of primitive sculpture which Weber had studied extensively in the museums in Paris and New York are reflected in this haunting woodcut, based on a painting of 1918, *The Worshiper* (private collection).

46
Rabbi Reading

1919–20
Color woodcut
4³⁄₁₆ x 1¹⁵⁄₁₆″ (106 x 49 mm)
Rubenstein 15
Purchased: Staunton B. Peck Fund
65-95-477

Weber's first wood block was cut with a penknife on the side of a box of honey he had received as a gift, a surface he liked so much that he continued to use honey boxes for some twenty-four more blocks in 1919 and 1920. He incorporated a crenelated edge of these boxes as a border in a number of his compositions, like this one of a rabbi reading, printed in simple, flat areas of color.

Edward Hopper

Nyack, New York 1882–1967 New York

Edward Hopper was one of America's most distinguished painters, known for his still, tellingly lit vignettes of America's urban and rural scene. He was also considered one of this country's finest printmakers. His formal art education began in 1899 with classes in illustrating, followed by six years at the New York School of Art studying painting under William Merritt Chase (q.v.), Kenneth Hayes Miller, and Robert Henri—and for a month with Henri's substitute John Sloan (q.v.). Between 1906 and 1910 Hopper made several trips abroad, spending much of his time in Paris, but also traveling extensively. He studied the art of the old masters, but it was the Impressionists—especially their handling of light—and Courbet and Daumier who most affected his work. Hopper exhibited paintings regularly in group shows in New York beginning in 1908, but he sold only one—*Sailing,* of 1911 (Carnegie Institute, Pittsburgh), from the Armory Show in 1913—before the Brooklyn Museum purchased *The Mansard Roof* in 1923. During this period he supported himself through commercial art, designing illustrations, advertisements, and covers for trade magazines; it was not until 1924 with the sale of an entire exhibition of his watercolors that he could give up this work to concentrate on painting.

In 1915 Hopper made the first of some seventy etchings and drypoints—landscapes, interiors, portraits, nudes, and sea views—imbued with the spirit of the graphic work of Rembrandt and Méryon. Although he received technical advice from his friend Martin Lewis (q.v.), he was largely self-taught, rapidly becoming a truly accomplished etcher. Hopper used etching as an expressive medium, developing his own style and working constantly with line to intensify his images through the contrast of light and dark areas. He was intensely concerned with quality, printing most of his plates himself. He searched for the whitest papers available and would even send to London for blacker inks to achieve a maximum brilliance. His prints were exhibited widely, receiving critical praise and awards; they also sold well long before his paintings did. In 1923, however, when he had begun to receive the attention for his watercolors and oils that would soon bring him world renown, he executed his last etching; his final drypoint was drawn in 1928.

The collection of Hopper prints in the Philadelphia Museum of Art, acquired by its first Curator of Prints, Carl Zigrosser, is extraordinary both in number and quality. Various states of almost every print are included as well as preparatory drawings for many of the images.

47

Night on the El Train

1918

Etching

$7\frac{3}{8}$ x $7\frac{15}{16}$" (187 x 201 mm)

Zigrosser 21

Purchased: Thomas Skelton Harrison Fund

62-19-21

This scene of a couple alone in a train on one of New York's elevated transit lines combines two subjects that recur in Hopper's work—the railroad and figures isolated in their environment.

48

Summer Afternoon

1919–23
Etching
7 7/16 x 7 13/16″ (189 x 199 mm)
Zigrosser 32
Purchased: Thomas Skelton Harrison Fund
62-19-32

Summer Afternoon is in the tradition of Impressionist boating scenes such as Mary Cassatt's *Boating Party* of 1893–94 (National Gallery of Art, Washington, D.C.).

49
American Landscape

1920
Etching
$7\frac{5}{16}$ x $12\frac{3}{8}$" (185 x 314 mm)
Zigrosser 1
Purchased: Thomas Skelton Harrison Fund
41-53-35

Hopper maintained the same studio on Washington Square in New York from 1913 until his death. Most summers, however, he vacationed on the coasts of Maine and Massachusetts, where he came in contact with—and depicted as he did here—rural America. The device of a horizontal landscape element at midground, repeated in many of his compositions, perhaps reflects the strong admiration that Hopper felt for Rembrandt's etchings.

50

House on a Hill (The Buggy)

1920
Etching
$7\frac{7}{8}$ x $9\frac{7}{8}$" (200 x 250 mm)
Zigrosser 14 VII/VII
Purchased: Thomas Skelton Harrison Fund
62-19-14(7)

The abruptly cutoff carriage in the foreground and the unusual viewpoint of this work owe much to the art of Degas and to photography.

51
Evening Wind

1921
Etching
6⅞ x 8¼″ (175 x 210 mm)
Zigrosser 9 VIII/VIII
Purchased: Thomas Skelton Harrison Fund
41-53-495

Hopper's *Evening Wind* has a precedent in Sloan's *Turning Out the Light* (no. 20), especially in its subject and its dramatic illumination from a single source.

52
Night in the Park

1921
Etching
$6^{13}/_{16}$ x $8^{1}/_{4}''$ (173 x 209 mm)
Zigrosser 20
Purchased: Thomas Skelton Harrison Fund
62-19-20(2)

The glow of the light falling from the streetlamp onto the newspaper and path, achieved through the clean wiping of unetched areas, picks out the solitary seated figure from the dense areas of deeply etched and heavily inked lines.

53
Night Shadows

1921
Etching
$6\frac{7}{8}$ x $8\frac{3}{16}$″ (175 x 208 mm)
Zigrosser 22 III/III
Purchased: Thomas Skelton Harrison Fund
62-19-22(3)

The vertical viewpoint, a device often exploited by the Impressionists in their boulevard scenes, and the long, curious shadow overwhelm the figure of a solitary man on an empty street.

54
East Side Interior

1922
Etching
$7^{13}/_{16}$ x $9^{15}/_{16}$" (199 x 252 mm)
Zigrosser 8 VI/VI
Purchased: Thomas Skelton Harrison Fund
41-53-496

Virtually all the details of many of Hopper's etchings were fully planned in preparatory drawings. But as the etchings proceeded, he often worked the plates through many states, progressively building up the hatching to increase the contrast between light and dark areas. Whereas the first state of this etching has a constant, almost even, illumination, this, the final state, shows a strong light that comes from the window and highlights areas with its brilliance while throwing the rest of the interior into dense shadow. In both its subject—a woman before an open window—and lighting, *East Side Interior* recalls seventeenth-century Dutch prints.

55
The Railroad

1922
Etching
$7^{13}/_{16}$ x $9^{13}/_{16}$" (199 x 249 mm)
Zigrosser 24 IX/IX
Purchased: Thomas Skelton Harrison Fund
62-19-24(9)

As in many Hopper etchings, the central element of the scene—here, the lone railroad switchman—would have been lost in the density of its surroundings had the contrast between the white areas and the heavily inked lines not defined the form so brilliantly.

56

The Lonely House

1923
Etching
$7^{13}/_{16}$ x $9^{13}/_{16}$" (199 x 249 mm)
Zigrosser 18
Purchased: Thomas Skelton Harrison Fund
62-19-18

Hopper's fascination with isolated figures became a repeated element in his later paintings. In *The Lonely House,* the figures dwarfed by architecture, as well as the deep, angular shadows and the flooding of light on a solid architectural surface, recall the street views of Paris etched by Méryon in the 1850s.

Arthur B. Davies

Utica, New York 1862–1928 Florence

Arthur B. Davies made his strongest impact on American art as the principal organizer of the Armory Show, the controversial exhibition that in 1913 brought the first large group of Cubist, Fauve, and other Post-Impressionist art to America. He was also a great collector and an adviser to those Americans whose collections would form the basis of the Museum of Modern Art in New York, founded in 1929. Davies's own painting was in a more personal idiom—rhythmic pastorals and female nudes, apart from the mainstream of American avant-garde art of his day and unlike the socially concerned paintings of many of The Eight, with whom he was associated.

By the time Davies settled in New York in 1887, he had studied with a local landscape painter in Utica, attended the Art Institute and the Academy of Design in Chicago, worked two years as a draftsman in Mexico, and traveled and sketched in the American West. He supported himself in New York as an illustrator, at the same time attending the Gotham Art School and the Art Students' League. Davies exhibited regularly after 1888, and he had his first one-man exhibition at the Macbeth Gallery in 1896, marking the start of his broader recognition. It was through his friendship with the gallery's owner, William Macbeth, that he had received financing for his first trip abroad in 1893, when he acted as Macbeth's agent, as he did again during his second trip in 1897. Davies saw a wide range of art in Europe, and his taste was catholic. He absorbed the lessons of Greek and Roman art, the Venetian painters, Botticelli, the Pre-Raphaelites, Whistler (q.v.), and Puvis de Chavannes; after the Armory Show, Cubism would also influence his work.

In 1908, Davies joined the group of artists who rebelled against the academic domination of the National Academy of Design and exhibited at the Macbeth Gallery as The Eight. It was as the president of another group also formed in reaction against the Academy, the Association of American Painters and Sculptors, that Davies later transformed an intended exhibition of contemporary American art into the sophisticated, international Armory Show.

Davies did not begin to concentrate on printmaking until about 1916, when he returned to the etching process with which he had experimented in the 1880s. He produced some two hundred works in etching, lithography, and mixed graphic techniques.

57
Ecstasy
1916*
Drypoint
3⅞ x 2¹⁵⁄₁₆" (99 x 74 mm)
Price 165 I/II
Purchased: Lola Downin Peck Fund from the Carl and Laura Zigrosser Collection
67-31-51

Davies's fascination with dancing figures is exemplified by this drypoint. Its variegated tonal background was achieved by the manipulation of ink on the plate.

* Information on dates and states of Davies's works is derived from Carl Zigrosser's annotations in a copy of Frederic Newlin Price, comp., *The Etchings & Lithographs of Arthur B. Davies* (New York, 1929), in the Philadelphia Museum of Art.

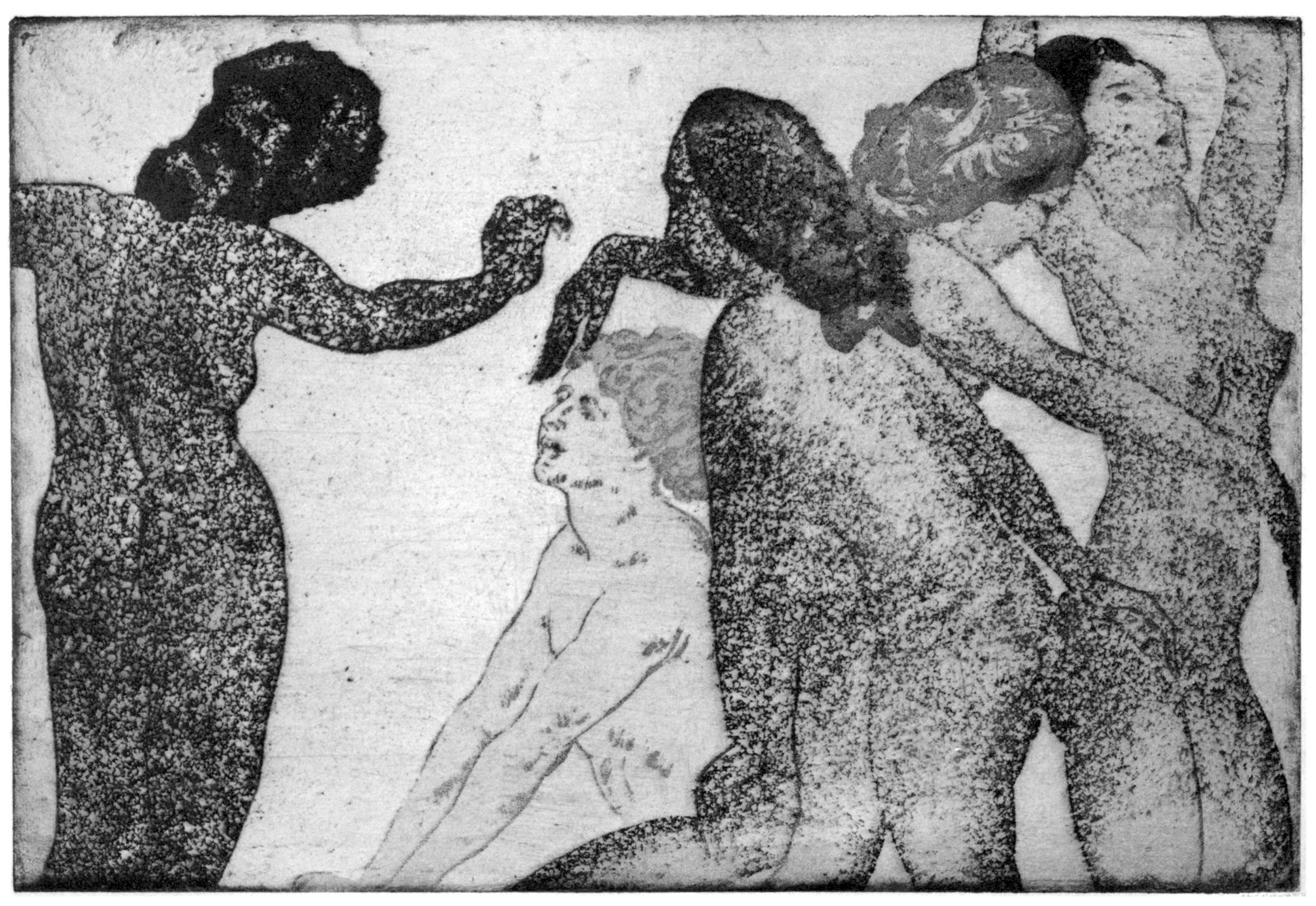

58
Valkyries
1919
Soft-ground etching and aquatint
$7^{13}/_{16}$ x $11^{7}/_{8}$" (199 x 302 mm)
Price 17 IV/V
Purchased: Lola Downin Peck Fund from the Carl and Laura Zigrosser Collection
67-31-9

Davies combined soft-ground etching and aquatint with two-toned printing to produce the varied effects of color, tone, and texture seen here.

59
Sea Maidens

1919–20
Aquatint
$7^{13}/_{16}$ x $7^{3}/_{8}''$ (198 x 188 mm)
Price 15 I/III
Gift of Carl Zigrosser
75-26-30

In articulating his artistic credo, Davies explained his compositional process: "I use a method of 'continuous composition'—repetition of the same motive. It is a subjective realization of a way used by the early Christian artist to preserve his original spontaneous subjectivity and oneness. . . ."*

* Quoted in Frederic Newlin Price, comp., *The Etchings & Lithographs of Arthur B. Davies* (New York, 1929), p. 19.

Lyonel Feininger

New York 1871–1956 New York

Lyonel Feininger is perhaps most widely recognized for his bold, intense woodcuts, which like his paintings and other prints are principally abstract architectural subjects rooted in Cubism, done during the fifty years he lived in Germany. Born in America of German ancestry, Feininger came from a family of musicians; he first went to Germany in 1887 to study music, but decided instead to become an artist, enrolling at the Kunstgewerbeschule in Hamburg, and then in 1888 at the academy in Berlin. Between 1890 and 1907 he worked as an illustrator and cartoonist, first for German publications, and later also under contract to the *Chicago Sunday Tribune,* where his two comic strips "The Kin-der-kids" and "Wee Willie Winkie's World" appeared weekly. In 1892–93 he studied at the Académie Colarossi in Paris, and his years in that city from 1906 to 1908 proved a turning point, for it was then that he gave up cartooning and decided to become a painter. In 1913 he was invited by the German painter Franz Marc to exhibit with the Blaue Reiter (Blue Rider) group in the first Herbstsalon in Berlin. His first one-man exhibition was held in 1917 at Der Sturm gallery in Berlin, and the next year he joined with a number of German Expressionists in forming the Socialist Novembergruppe, which eventually became incorporated into the Bauhaus movement. In 1919 he was chosen to become the first master at the Bauhaus and soon was put in charge of its graphic workshop. He continued his association with the Bauhaus until the government closed it in 1933. The esteem accorded Feininger in a large retrospective exhibition held at the Nationalgalerie in Berlin in 1931 did not last as Nazi power strengthened; in 1937 his work was included in the "degenerate art" exhibition in Munich. That year he returned permanently to the United States.

Feininger produced more than 300 woodcuts, some 65 etchings and drypoints, and 20 lithographs. He had begun to make lithographs and drypoints in 1906, but he did not cut his first wood block until 1918, when the First World War caused severe shortages of painting supplies and metal printing plates in Germany. During the first year alone he made 117 wood-block prints. He found in this medium the freedom to establish a new style, drawing on the woodcuts of the German Expressionists, and the ability to print his own works readily, thus bypassing the complicated procedures of pulling proofs in etching and lithography.

60
The Gate

1912
Etching and drypoint
10$^{11}/_{16}$ x 7$^{13}/_{16}$″ (272 x 198 mm)
Prasse E52
Gift of Carl Zigrosser
66-226-5

The Gate is one of the earliest works in which the impact of Cubism on Feininger can be seen. The whimsical figures, however, are more closely allied to the style of his earlier cartoons.

61

Mellingen

1919
Woodcut
$11^{15}/_{16}$ x 10″ (303 x 254 mm)
Prasse W185 II/II
Print Club Permanent Collection
51-59-6

Mellingen is one of the villages in the central German region of Thuringia that inspired many of Feininger's works for over two decades.

62

Villa on the Shore, 4

1920
Woodcut
$10^{9}/_{16}$ x $13^{7}/_{16}$″ (268 x 341 mm)
Prasse W226
Print Club Permanent Collection
45-48-21

In this woodcut of the kaiser's villa at the Baltic seaside resort of Heringsdorf, Feininger set the classical house against pyramidal hills under a mysteriously illuminated sky. Feininger experimented with the quality, texture, and color of papers, often using several different types for printing a single image. This impression is printed on fine tissue.

John Marin

Rutherford, New Jersey 1870–1953
Cape Split, Maine

John Marin did not become a professional artist until he had reached his mid-thirties, but he quickly established a reputation as an etcher and watercolorist. After drifting in and out of jobs, including four years spent in architects' offices and several years of desultory study at the Pennsylvania Academy of the Fine Arts in Philadelphia and the Art Students' League in New York, Marin went to Paris in 1905 with the financial aid of his family. Immediately he began to etch, using the press and tools of his stepbrother, an artist resident in Paris, and teaching himself the rudiments of the process from Maxime Lalanne's *Treatise on Etching* (Roxbury, Mass., 1880), which he had purchased in New York. Within three months after his arrival he had executed twelve etchings of Paris, one of which was successfully published, and he continued to etch views of the city in the manner of Whistler (q.v.); visits to Amsterdam (1906), Laon (1906), Venice (1907), and Germany (1910) provided other subjects for his work. Through his friendship with the photographer Edward Steichen, an exhibition of his watercolors was held at Alfred Stieglitz's "291" gallery in New York in 1909. That same year Marin met Stieglitz in Paris, and Stieglitz devoted an entire exhibition to his European watercolors, pastels, and etchings in 1910. Armed with a guarantee of financial support from Stieglitz, Marin returned to New York, and he began to view the vital, rapidly growing city as his primary subject. He developed a totally new expressionistic approach—intense, semi-abstract views of angular, fragmented structures, influenced by Cézanne and Cubism—producing among his finest works etchings of the Brooklyn Bridge and the Woolworth Building. In 1914, Marin began to spend his summers on the coast of Maine, where he painted dynamic watercolors of the sea, sky, and mountains, which he exhibited regularly at Stieglitz's successive New York galleries.

The Philadelphia Museum of Art owns a comprehensive collection of John Marin's 180 etchings, including a large number of rare and unique impressions; the majority of the works were acquired from the artist's estate.

63
Notre Dame, Paris

1908
Etching
12 9/16 x 10 5/8" (319 x 270 mm)
Zigrosser 79 v/v
The J. Wolfe Golden and Celeste Golden Collection of John Marin Etchings
69-81-63

No etcher of this era could be free from Whistler's pervasive influence, which was to endure long after the artist's death in 1903. Marin emulated Whistler in this atmospherically diffused and geometrically patterned view of Notre Dame but recalled the engraver Charles Méryon in his choice of subject.

NOTRE-DAME PARIS

64
Woolworth Building, No. 1

1913
Etching
$11^{13}/_{16}$ x $9^{7}/_{8}$" (300 x 251 mm)
Zigrosser 113
The J. Wolfe Golden and Celeste Golden Collection of John Marin Etchings
69-81-86

Marin was fascinated with the many new landmarks and the frenzied construction work he found on his return to New York. In 1913, the year he executed this expressionistic view of the Woolworth Building, he wrote an interpretive note about his Manhattan subjects then being shown at "291":

"The whole city is alive; buildings, people, all are alive; and the more they move me the more I feel them to be alive.

"It is this 'moving of me' that I try to express, so that I may recall the spell I have been under and behold the expression of the different emotions that have been called into being. . . .

"In life all things come under the magnetic influence of other things; the bigger assert themselves strongly, the smaller not so much, but still they assert themselves, and though hidden they strive to be seen and in so doing change their bent and direction."*

The tones in the sky and the cityscape were achieved by the selective wiping and scraping of ink on the plate. The addition of emphatic dark areas directly with the fingertips (most apparent at lower left) gives an intense, dramatic effect to a rather sparsely etched print.

* Quoted in *Camera Work,* nos. 42–43 (April–July 1913), p. 18.

65

Brooklyn Bridge, No. 6 (Swaying)

1913
Etching
10⅝ x 8 11/16″ (270 x 221 mm)
Zigrosser 112
Purchased: Lola Downin Peck Fund from the Carl and Laura Zigrosser Collection
67-31-99

Marin examined the great jungle of cables and the monumental structure of the Brooklyn Bridge from many angles and viewpoints. This view of 1913 was published by Stieglitz and sold as one of Marin's *Six New York Etchings.*

66

Movement—Grain Elevators, No. 1

1916
Etching
$7^{13/16}$ x $9^{5/8}$" (199 x 244 mm)
Zigrosser 127 I/II
The J. Wolfe Golden and Celeste Golden Collection of John Marin Etchings
69-81-96

In this essay into almost complete abstraction, Marin expressed with great economy of etched lines the angles and forces of grain elevators. Inked pieces of rubber pressed on the plate before printing provided the tonal areas that give tone and solidity to the composition.

67

Downtown, the El

1921
Etching
$6\frac{3}{4}$ x $8\frac{9}{16}''$ (171 x 218 mm)
Zigrosser 134
The J. Wolfe Golden and Celeste Golden Collection of John Marin Etchings
69-81-104

Marin treated this same subject in two previous, somewhat more naturalistic, etchings. Here, with rapidly drawn lines, he conveyed a sense of motion, eliminating details from the earlier versions, such as a horse and carriage (barely suggested at right), windows in the skyscrapers, and structural details of the elevated transit line.

68
Sailboat

1932
Etching
$6\frac{7}{8}$ x $9\frac{1}{4}$″ (174 x 234 mm)
Zigrosser 155
Gift of Carl Zigrosser
72-237-15

In this print of a sailboat executed eighteen years after he had discovered Maine, Marin for the first time etched a subject he had investigated repeatedly in watercolors and oils.

69
Yachts

1924
Lithograph
$7\frac{15}{16}$ x $9\frac{7}{8}$″ (201 x 251 mm)
The Louise and Walter Arensberg Collection
50-134-C-913

Sheeler's study of yachts in full sail retains the soft and spacious quality of the crayon drawing of about 1922 on which this lithograph is based (Whitney Museum of American Art, New York).

Charles Sheeler

Philadelphia 1883–1965 Dobbs Ferry, New York

The painter and photographer Charles Sheeler studied applied art at the Pennsylvania School of Industrial Art in Philadelphia (1900–1903) and learned to paint in a broad, rapid style under William Merritt Chase (q.v.) at the Pennsylvania Academy of the Fine Arts (1903–6). During the summers of 1904 and 1905 he traveled with Chase's class to Europe, noting especially the seventeenth-century Spanish and Dutch artists who had been so important in shaping his teacher's art. Sheeler returned to Europe in 1909, traveling to Italy and France, where he studied the Italian Renaissance artists and saw the canvases of Cézanne, the Cubists, and the Fauves, whose deliberate organization of reality would affect his painting style over the next decade. About 1912 he became a photographer, and an exhibition of his photographs was held at Marius de Zayas's Modern Gallery in New York in 1918, two years before his paintings were in a one-man exhibition, also at de Zayas's gallery.

During these years Sheeler came into contact with leaders of the artistic and intellectual avant-garde as a frequent visitor to the New York salon of Walter and Louise Arensberg, whose collection of the art of this period is now in the Philadelphia Museum of Art. His work, primarily rural and industrial subjects, became increasingly abstract and architectonic, executed with the clarity, austerity, and exactitude that made him a central figure among the American Precisionists—the name applied to a number of painters of the urban and industrial scene, including Louis Lozowick, Niles Spencer (qq.v.), Charles Demuth, Georgia O'Keeffe, and Joseph Stella. Beginning in the early 1920s, his paintings, photographs, and drawings were widely collected and exhibited as Sheeler gained national and international fame. His few lithographs, mostly executed in the 1920s, were done to explore the formalism of his drawing style.

70
Delmonico Building

1927
Lithograph
$9\frac{3}{4}$ x $6\frac{11}{16}$" (247 x 170 mm)
The Louise and Walter Arensberg Collection
50-134-C-914

This lithograph marks Sheeler's earliest artistic use of an upward view in which buildings seem to converge, a device he had learned from photography and used repeatedly in the film *Manahatta,* which he made with the photographer Paul Strand in 1920.

71
Industrial Series, No. 1

1928
Lithograph
$8\frac{1}{8}$ x $11\frac{1}{16}$" (207 x 281 mm)
Purchased: Lola Downin Peck Fund from the Carl and Laura Zigrosser Collection
74-24-200

In 1927, the Ford Motor Company commissioned Sheeler to photograph its River Rouge plant near Detroit as a document of the power and majesty of American industry.* Sheeler's series of thirty-two photographs of the then-largest industrial complex in the world, covering over two thousand acres and employing seventy-five thousand workers, reveals the formal purity and underlying functionalism of the industrial site. These photographs inspired a number of drawings, watercolors, and oils, many with idealized titles such as *Classic Landscape* and *Ballet Mechanique.* This lithograph is based on a watercolor now in the Carnegie Institute's Museum of Art (Pittsburgh). Sheeler painted an oil of the same subject in 1930 (Museum of Modern Art, New York).

* *See* Detroit, The Detroit Institute of Arts, *The Rouge: The Image of Industry in the Art of Charles Sheeler and Diego Rivera* (August 15–November 1, 1978), pp. 7–17, 32–38.

72
Roses

c. 1924
Lithograph
11$\frac{1}{8}$ x 9$\frac{3}{16}$″ (282 x 233 mm)
The Louise and Walter Arensberg Collection
50-134-C-912

Sheeler executed a number of flower studies which, like this richly toned lithograph, all show the same photographic clarity imposed on his landscapes.

Marsden Hartley

Lewiston, Maine 1877–1943
Ellsworth, Maine

Marsden Hartley's stylistically varied artistic work culminated in the richly colored canvases of coastal Maine for which he is best known today. Born and raised in Maine, as a teen-ager Hartley moved to Cleveland where he studied at the Cleveland School of Art (1898). After moving to New York, he became a pupil of William Merritt Chase (q.v.) at the New York School of Art (1899–1900) and attended classes at the National Academy of Design (1900–1904). Hartley's early canvases painted in an Impressionist style were shown in his first one-man exhibition, at Alfred Stieglitz's "291" gallery in 1909. Traveling abroad in 1912–15, he lived first in Paris and then in Germany, where he exhibited with the Blaue Reiter (Blue Rider) group in Munich and at the first Herbstsalon in Berlin. It was during these years that his work began to undergo the successive changes in style that would occur over the next decade. Paintings in a Fauve manner were followed by patterned expressionistic abstractions with German military symbols, then by Cubist compositions, but by 1920 he returned to more naturalistic subjects and he began to concentrate on landscapes, especially those of Maine. Hartley's print activity was limited to some seventeen lithographs executed in two separate series in Germany: still lifes of fruit and flowers in 1922–23, and views of the Bavarian Alps in 1933–34.

73
Bowl of Fruit
1923
Lithograph
12 7/16 x 11 15/16" (316 x 304 mm)
Purchased: Thomas Skelton Harrison Fund
41-53-31

From Hartley's first group of lithographs, which were probably transferred to the stone and printed by a professional, this bold, broadly defined bowl of fruit is set on a tilted tabletop, a device that may be found in still lifes by Cézanne and the Fauves.

Niles Spencer

Pawtucket, Rhode Island 1893–1952
Dingman's Ferry, Pennsylvania

Niles Spencer's austere images of cities and factories associate him with the Precisionists, who through the clarity of their rendering and the simplicity of their design brought stature to the depiction of the industrial and technological environment. Spencer studied at the Rhode Island School of Design from 1913 to 1915, and then in New York in 1915 and 1916 with the painter and educator Kenneth Hayes Miller at the Art Students' League and with Robert Henri and George Bellows (q.v.) at the Ferrer School. He settled in New York in 1917, spending his summers in Maine and Massachusetts. Spencer's first journey abroad was in 1921–22, when he was impressed with the paintings of the Italian Primitives, Cézanne, and the Cubists. He had one-man shows at the Daniel Gallery in New York in 1925 and 1928. In his Precisionist paintings, like his lithographs, the simplified volumes and architectural planes are generally presented without reference to human activity or anecdotal detail.

74
White Factory
1928
Lithograph
$10\frac{5}{8} \times 13\frac{9}{16}$" (269 x 344 mm)
Purchased: Lola Downin Peck Fund from the Carl and Laura Zigrosser Collection

Using a vocabulary inspired by Cubism, Spencer charged his composition with a tension created by the interplay of solid structures with textured and patterned surfaces.

Louis Lozowick

Ludvinovka, Russia 1892–1973 South Orange, New Jersey

Louis Lozowick is best known for his lithographs, especially the compositions of cities, industrial projects, and workers he executed in the late 1920s and 1930s. Having immigrated to the United States in 1906, he studied at the National Academy of Design in New York from 1912 to 1915 and was graduated from Ohio State University in 1918. An extended trip across the country in 1919 and 1920 inspired his "Cities" series, paintings done from memory that he began only after he had arrived in Paris in 1921 and which would become the basis for his first essays into lithography around 1923. In Berlin from 1922 to 1924, Lozowick became known for his paintings with American themes, his artistic renown probably spurred by the European fascination with America's dynamic technological strides. A member of the Socialist Novembergruppe, Lozowick also became familiar with a group of avant-garde Russian artists living in Berlin, among them the Constructivist El Lissitzky, and he met others including Vladimir Tatlin and Kasimir Malevich on a short trip to Russia in 1922. His study of their work, *Modern Russian Art* (New York, 1925), is still considered a standard source in this field. The impact on Lozowick of the Constructivists' geometric abstractions and machine aesthetic is particularly apparent in his series of "Machine Ornament" drawings, which were exhibited along with his "Cities" series in a one-man exhibition in New York in 1926. After his return to America in 1924, Lozowick began to use lithography as his most important medium. About 1926, at the time he joined the staff of the left-wing magazine *The New Masses* as a writer and an illustrator, his art began to shift from generalized, formal compositions of cities and machines done in a Precisionist manner toward a more naturalistic approach and a more human scale. Visits to the Soviet Union in 1928 (when he exhibited twenty-eight works, including three lithographs, in a one-man show at the Museum of Western Art in Moscow) and in 1931 intensified his increasing focus on workers and social concerns. During the Depression, he did graphics, paintings, and murals for the Work Projects Administration (WPA).

75
New York

1925
Lithograph
11 9/16 x 9 1/16" (294 x 230 mm)
Purchased: Lola Downin Peck Fund from the Carl and Laura Zigrosser Collection
1980-3-133

Between 1922 and 1927, Lozowick transferred some of his earlier "Cities" paintings into pencil drawings and lithographs. Among the cities he represented were Chicago, Cleveland, Minneapolis, and New York—shown here in a futuristic reconstitution of the essence of the metropolis, empty however of its population.

76
Subway Construction

1931
Lithograph
6⅝ x 13″ (169 x 330 mm)
Purchased: Lola Downin Peck Fund from the Carl and Laura Zigrosser Collection
1980-3-131

In his lithographs of the late 1920s and early 1930s, Lozowick turned his attention from Precisionist views of cities and factories devoid of humanity to more naturalistic scenes in which workers are represented within their environment.

77
Brooklyn Bridge

1930
Lithograph
13 x 7⅞″ (330 x 200 mm)
Anonymous gift
42-56-6

In an essay, "The Americanization of Art," included in the catalogue of the *Machine Age Exposition* held in New York in 1927, Lozowick explained his style and choice of subject:

"The dominant trend in America of Today, beneath all the apparent chaos and confusion is towards order and organization which find their outward sign and symbol in the rigid geometry of the American city: in the verticals of its smoke stacks, in the parallels of its car tracks, the squares of its streets, the cubes of its factories, the arc of its bridges, the cylinders of its gas tanks.

"Upon this underlying mathematical pattern as a scaffolding may be built a solid plastic structure of great intricacy and subtlety. The artist who confronts his task with original vision and accomplished craftsmanship, will note with exactitude the articulation, solidity, and weight of advancing and receding masses, will define with precision the space around objects and between them; he will organize line, plane and volume into a well knit design, arrange color and light into a pattern of contrast and harmony and weave organically into every composition an all pervading rhythm and equilibrium. . . ."*

* Quoted in Burlington, Vt., The University of Vermont, Robert Hull Fleming Museum, *Abstraction and Realism: 1923–1943. Paintings, Drawings, and Lithographs of Louis Lozowick* (March 14–April 18, 1971), cover.

78
Still Life, No. 2

1929
Lithograph
$10\frac{1}{4}$ x $13\frac{1}{8}$" (260 x 334 mm)
Purchased: Lola Downin Peck Fund from the Carl and Laura Zigrosser Collection
1980-3-89

The same precision and geometric rigidity which Lozowick imposed on American architectural monuments were applied to his still lifes. Here the extreme viewpoint of this crisply defined and sharply contrasted composition is accentuated by the elongated shadows cast by each of the isolated objects.

Stuart Davis

Philadelphia 1894–1964 New York

Although he did not study abroad, Stuart Davis was among the first Americans to embrace modernism, when after seeing the 1913 Armory Show he resolved that he "would quite definitely have to become a 'modern' artist."* Well acquainted with artists from his youth—as art editor of the *Philadelphia Press* his father had many artist friends and had employed several members of The Eight—Davis left high school to study at Robert Henri's school in New York (1910–13), painting in the realist idiom of the "Ashcan" painters. From 1913 to 1916, he worked for the Socialist magazine *The Masses* under its art director John Sloan (q.v.), and drew cartoons for *Harper's Weekly*. After the Armory Show, at which he himself exhibited five watercolors, he struggled to assimilate the ideas of the European modernists into his work as he developed his own style. Elements of van Gogh, Gauguin, the Cubists, the Expressionists, Matisse, and the Fauves all may be traced in his experimental work of the next decades; he began to simplify his paintings, denying illusionistic space and fragmenting the visual world into colorful, abstracted compositions. Davis spent a year abroad in 1928–29, executing a series of flattened views of Paris streets in oil and in lithography; a number of lithographs with American subjects followed his return to New York. During the 1930s Davis worked for the Work Projects Administration (WPA) in New York as a muralist and was active in the Artists' Union and Artists' Congress. By the late 1930s, he had arrived at the brilliant abstractions, vibrating with rhythms and punctuated with typography, that established him as a unique figure in American art.

* Quoted in James Johnson Sweeney, *Stuart Davis* (New York, 1945), p. 10.

79
Rue des Rats

1928
Lithograph
10 1/16 x 15 3/16" (256 x 386 mm)
Purchased: Thomas Skelton Harrison Fund
41-53-16

In Paris in 1928–29, Davis executed a series of black-and-white lithographs of street scenes and paintings of the same subjects. Here, Davis used a rapid crosshatching to convey a sense of the texture that he achieved with rough impasto in the corresponding canvas, *Rue des Rats, No. 2*, of 1929 (private collection).

80

Sixth Avenue El

1931
Lithograph
$11\frac{15}{16} \times 17\frac{13}{16}''$ (303 x 453 mm)
Purchased: Thomas Skelton Harrison Fund
43-2-175

In 1931 Davis executed two lithographs of New York's Sixth Avenue elevated train line using a number of disparate elements in collagelike juxtapositions to reconstruct a view of the station at Eighth Street in Greenwich Village. In this lithograph Davis combined the columns, overhead light, and chewing-gum vending machine of the train platform with fragments from the surrounding neighborhood—sewing machines and dress forms from tailor shops, a barber pole, and the Star of David and the Hebrew word "kosher" from a Jewish butcher shop. In the center is what appears to be the tower of the Jefferson Market Courthouse, the same structure seen in the distance in John Sloan's view of the Sixth Avenue el from his studio (no. 26).

81

Barber Shop Chord

1931
Lithograph
14 x 18 15/16″ (335 x 481 mm)
Purchased: Thomas Skelton Harrison Fund
43-2-176

Davis spent most summers between 1915 and 1934 in the fishing village of Gloucester, Massachusetts, which appeared frequently in his work. This lithograph offers an intriguing insight into Davis's working method. The various elements were abstracted from a representational view of a New England dockside street in a gouache of 1929 (Whitney Museum of American Art, New York); here only the surrealistic figure has been added, as if on center stage against a flattened backdrop.

Rockwell Kent

Tarrytown, New York 1882–1971
Plattsburgh, New York

The fine quality of Rockwell Kent's wood engraving places him in the forefront of the many American artists working in this medium in the 1920s and 1930s. His book illustrations—notably those for the works of Shakespeare, Chaucer, Herman Melville, and Walt Whitman—advertising designs, and murals, as well as his paintings and drawings brought him great popularity in America until the late 1940s, when he fell out of favor because of his leftist ideology. After studying architecture at Columbia University from 1900 to 1902, Kent took up painting, working in New York successively under William Merritt Chase (q.v.), Robert Henri, Kenneth Hayes Miller, and the landscape painter Abbott H. Thayer. His first one-man exhibition was held in New York in 1907, when he showed paintings done on Monhegan Island, Maine, where he had been living. He joined with Henri in organizing an independent exhibition at the time of the spring show of the National Academy of Design in 1910, and he was associated with George Bellows, John Steuart Curry (qq.v.), and members of The Eight, exhibiting with them at the Whitney Studio Club before 1920. Kent's prints—primarily wood engravings and lithographs, begun about 1918—stand apart from the socially concerned realistic depictions of daily life favored by his contemporaries; his own political beliefs and social consciousness were expressed through broader symbols—especially the idealized male figure—as well as through his many published statements. Kent's extensive travels in New England, Greenland, Alaska, and Tierra del Fuego are documented in a number of his illustrated books. An exhibition in honor of his seventy-fifth birthday was held at the Hermitage in Leningrad and the Pushkin Museum in Moscow, and in 1960 he presented a large collection of his paintings, drawings, and prints to the Soviet Union. Kent was awarded the Lenin Peace Prize in 1967.

The Philadelphia Museum of Art houses a major collection of Rockwell Kent drawings and prints as well as several original wood blocks and lithographic stones.

82
Starlight
1930
Wood engraving
5 5/16 x 6 7/8" (135 x 174 mm)
Zigrosser 42, Burne Jones 52
Anonymous gift
41-49-2

The strong solitary figure silhouetted against the sky in a landscape charged with symbolism if not mysticism is a hallmark of Kent's work. In his autobiography, however, Kent disclaimed any mystical intention:

"In many of my engravings and lithographs . . . people have inclined to find a mystic quality that is so obviously at variance with my own proclaimed belief in realism, and my fundamental disbelief in Deity, as to deserve consideration. Mysticism . . . is premised on the belief in an omnipresent unifying principle or spirit that by its own illusiveness is indefinable and inaccessible to understanding. I believe that all things can, and some day will, be understood. I believe in Man as the supreme consciousness; and in the arts as the supreme expression of his spirit."*

Starlight is one of Kent's series of twelve wood engravings commissioned by the American Car and Foundry Company for reproduction as magazine advertisements during 1930 and 1931.

* Rockwell Kent, *It's Me O Lord* (New York, 1955), pp. 423–24.

83
The Lovers

1928
Wood engraving
$6\frac{1}{2}$ x $10\frac{1}{16}$" (165 x 256 mm)
Zigrosser 23, Burne Jones 23
Purchased: Lola Downin Peck Fund from the Carl and Laura Zigrosser Collection
71-2-315

Typical of Kent's wood-engraving style are his extreme contrasts of flat black-and-white areas, with line used sparingly, as here, to give solidity to the figures and to define detail selectively.

84

Revisitation

1928
Lithograph
8 7/16 x 13 5/8" (214 x 346 mm)
Zigrosser 22, Burne Jones 22
Purchased: Lola Downin Peck Fund from the Carl and Laura Zigrosser Collection
71-2-258

In *How I Make a Woodcut* (Pasadena, Calif., 1934), Kent explained how his experiences with nature inspired his art in a passage that could in fact describe his work on this print:

"Almost every Sunday night in summer, here in the Adirondack mountains, we . . . go upon a picnic. Our picnic ground is invariably a certain field of an abandoned mountain farm, from which, seated among those memorials of man's transitory tenure on earth, the moss grown stones of old foundations, we contemplate those universal symbols of immutability: the mountains and the starlit heavens. Yet so happy are the auspices, each other's company, under which we there convene, and so vast the self containedness of the immensity that is our spectacle, that we are under no constraint to solemn mood. . . . The firelight, the darkness and the stars: no wonder if to some of us there comes the recollection of some poet's lines; or to another merely 'Gee, it's swell'; or that some other with a soul 'not less therefore divine' says nothing and thinks less, content—but singularly so—to be. No wonder if the recollections of the night remain; nor that Monday morning finds the artist of the party re-invoking to himself its mood and trying with his pencil to recapture it.

"Yet the problem is not alone the re-creation of those natural elements of last night's scene—night, mountains, stones, and stars—that has so moved him, but of the mood itself, how man reacted there that night to that environment. This is the problem, and he draws—a man."*

* Quoted in Dan Burne Jones, *The Prints of Rockwell Kent* (Chicago, 1975), p. xiv.

Martin Lewis

Castlemaine, Australia 1881–1962
New York

Martin Lewis was widely praised in his lifetime for his graphic technique and his ability to capture New York in its various moods and at various times of day. A devoted craftsman, he conveyed effects of light, atmosphere, and tone, not like Whistler and his followers by the inking and selective wiping of the plate, but through the working of line alone. The 143 prints that he made between 1915 and 1949 are mostly picturesque scenes of New York, where he lived for some fifty years. Lewis came to the United States from Australia in 1900, settling in New York the next year and beginning a career as a commercial artist, which he continued until the late 1920s. He made his first print in 1915 and very soon began to experiment with a range of intaglio processes—etching, drypoint, aquatint, and mezzotint—ultimately favoring drypoint because he could achieve dense velvety blacks and at the same time manipulate the technique to create fine gradations of gray. The influence of photography and of Japanese prints, the latter with which he became familiar on a trip to Japan in 1920–22, may be felt in his work. In 1934 he organized a printmaking school in New York with the lithographer George Miller and the printmaker Armin Landeck, and Lewis taught at the Art Students' League from 1944 to 1951.

85
Stoops in Snow

1930
Drypoint with sandpaper ground
9 15/16 x 15″ (253 x 381 mm)
Kennedy Galleries 95
Staunton B. Peck Bequest
46-2-17

Lewis's fascination with varying light and weather conditions is reflected repeatedly throughout his work, a debt to Japanese art, photography, and Impressionism. His concern for contemporaneity has made his prints documentary pieces of his era.

86

Glow of the City

1929
Drypoint
$11\frac{5}{16}$ x $14\frac{3}{8}$" (288 x 365 mm)
Kennedy Galleries 87
Print Club Permanent Collection
42-52-64

Here Lewis has contrasted the lifestyles of New York—the dark tenements of the poor with the glowing tower of big business—perhaps offering some hope for the future in this symbolic print.

87

Quarter of Nine, Saturday's Children

1929
Drypoint
10 x 12$^{13}/_{16}$″ (254 x 326 mm)
Kennedy Galleries 88
Gift of the Estate of Mrs. Charles M. Lea
47-9-11

In this scene of shopgirls hurrying to work, Lewis achieved a remarkable effect of early morning light through his concentration on line. This technique was the essence of his craft, as he explained in 1928: "The essential qualities of a good print may be considered as brilliancy of impression, purity and definite intention of line. Many modern etchers attempt to get by manipulation of the printing, effects that should be obtained legitimately by work on the plate itself."*

*Quoted in New York, Kennedy Galleries, *Martin Lewis: The Graphic Work* (April 11–28, 1973), n.p.

88

Relics

1928
Drypoint
$11\frac{7}{8}$ x $9\frac{15}{16}$" (301 x 252 mm)
Kennedy Galleries 65
Staunton B. Peck Bequest
50-103-112

Edward Hopper (q.v.) and Martin Lewis were lifelong friends, and it was Lewis who around 1915 gave Hopper pointers about the technique of etching. There can be little doubt that Hopper's etching *Night Shadows* of 1921 (no. 53) was the prototype for this nighttime image by Lewis, similarly lit by a single light, drawn from a high viewpoint, and having long, prominent shadows.

89

The Bowery

1928
Lithograph
$8\frac{1}{4}$ x $11\frac{11}{16}$" (209 x 297 mm)
Sasowsky 16
Purchased: Thomas Skelton Harrison Fund
41-53-42

Most of Marsh's thirty-four lithographs were executed in Paris on two separate trips, in 1928 and 1932; drawn in his illustration style, they were printed as *chines collés.* This lithograph of derelicts loitering in the shadow of the el that then straddled the Bowery was printed in Paris, but must have been done from sketches drawn in New York. A similar drawing was used as an illustration in *The New Yorker* on October 20,1928, with the caption, "Oh, Al Smith's all right, but I'm fer leaving prosperity alone," a reference to the campaign of the Democratic presidential candidate Al Smith.

Reginald Marsh

Paris 1898–1954 Dorset, Vermont

Reginald Marsh is best known for his images of New York—its subways and streets, its burlesque houses and amusement parks, Coney Island and the Bowery—viewed with an observant eye but not without a measure of both sympathy and satire. Born in Paris to American artists, Marsh was introduced early to the world of art and drew constantly as a child. He grew up in comfortable surroundings, attending private schools and taking a degree at Yale University. In 1920 he went to New York, where he worked as an illustrator for newspapers and magazines; his longest associations were with the *New York Daily News* (1922–25), where he drew illustrations of vaudeville acts, and with *The New Yorker* (beginning in 1925). He studied for short periods at the Art Students' League, which included a night class in drawing with John Sloan (q.v.). Around 1923, he began to paint seriously and joined the New York center for independent artists, the Whitney Studio Club, where he had his first one-man show in 1924. In 1925–26 and 1928, Marsh was in Europe studying and copying the work of the old masters; their emphasis on form, structure, and draftsmanship was reinforced for Marsh in his classes with Kenneth Hayes Miller at the Art Students' League in 1927–28. Marsh saw anatomy as the basis of his art: he dissected corpses at medical schools and drew from the model regularly, later publishing his own work on the subject, *Anatomy for Artists* (New York, 1945). During the 1930s Marsh worked as a muralist under the Treasury Department Art Program, completing frescoes for the Post Office Department Building in Washington, D.C., and a large mural cycle for the rotunda of the United States Customs House in New York.

It was Marsh's practice to turn to printmaking in the evening, when the light in his studio on Union Square was no longer suitable for painting; he was often able to crystallize in black and white and on a small scale, the subjects he treated in other mediums. Largely self-taught as a printmaker—although in 1940 he did study engraving with Stanley William Hayter—he looked to Rembrandt, Daumier, Goya, Hogarth, and Rowlandson for inspiration and to his immediate predecessors in New York, Sloan, Hopper, and Bellows (qq.v.), for direct models. Marsh made his first etching in Paris in 1926 and his first lithograph, also in Paris, in 1928. He concentrated on etching during the 1930s, turning increasingly to engraving later in the decade. Marsh executed a total of some 236 lithographs, etchings, and engravings.

90
Merry-Go-Round

1930
Etching and engraving
$6\frac{7}{8} \times 9\frac{13}{16}''$ (175 x 249 mm)
Sasowsky 99 VI/VI
Purchased: Lola Downin Peck Fund from the Carl and Laura Zigrosser Collection
74-24-142

Along with his patronage of burlesque houses, Marsh frequented amusement parks, where the rides forced the fun seekers into strange attitudes to be viewed from unusual angles. His concentration here is on the frenzied riders and their agitated horses, highly modeled figures filling the entire surface of the print.

91

Steeplechase

1932
Etching and engraving
$7^{13}/_{16}$ x $10^{7}/_{8}$″ (199 x 277 mm)
Sasowsky 138 x/x
Purchased: Thomas Skelton Harrison Fund
41-53-483

Coney Island's Steeplechase Park, a large structure filled with rides and arcades, is the scene of most of Marsh's amusement-park compositions. Its name came from this steeplechase ride of racing steeds on iron rails encircling the park.

92
Irving Place Burlesk

1930
Etching and engraving
$9^{15}/_{16}$ x 12″ (253 x 305 mm)
Sasowsky 101 VIII/VIII
Gift of Reginald Marsh
41-94-4

The burlesque was among Marsh's most frequent subjects; he used the striptease as an excuse to include a voluptuous nude figure in a scene from real life rather than painting the nude in an idealized academic setting. But Marsh also saw social relevance in this subject, feeling that the "burlesque show is a very sad commentary on the state of the poor man. It is the only entertainment, the only presentation of sex that he can afford. . . . As for painting it, the whole thing is extremely pictorial. You get a woman in the spotlight, the gilt architecture of the place, plenty of humanity. Everything is nice and intimate, not spread out and remote as in a regular theater."* In 1930 Marsh also painted this same scene (private collection), and he earlier had executed a lithograph and two etchings entitled *Irving Place Burlesk.* This etching is the most finished and successful of the prints.

* Quoted in Lloyd Goodrich, *Reginald Marsh* (New York, 1972), p. 37.

93
Tattoo—Shave—Haircut

1932
Etching
9$\frac{11}{16}$ x 9$\frac{11}{16}$″ (246 x 246 mm)
Sasowsky 140 x/x
Purchased: Thomas Skelton Harrison Fund
41-53-486

Tattoo—Shave—Haircut is Marsh's most famous and successful print. As in a number of his extremely powerful images, the highly modeled figures exist in a shallow space, almost like a relief, here set against a tawdry street beneath the el on New York's Lower East Side. Its dense overall tonality built up of tightly drawn and richly inked lines unites this scene into a fantastic vision of the seaminess of city life. A painting of the same design, *Tattoo and Haircut,* of 1932, is in the Art Institute of Chicago.

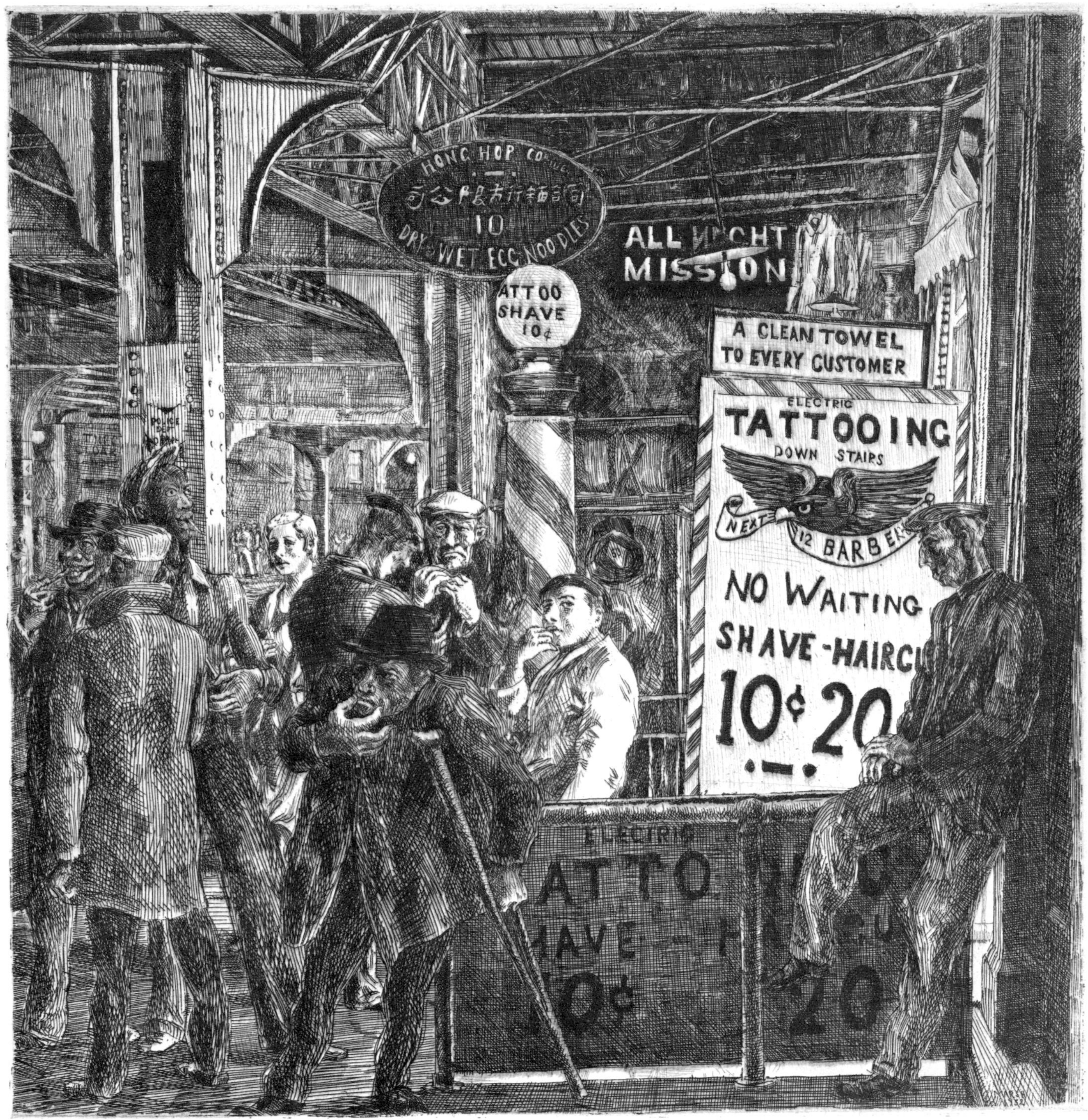

94
Coney Island Beach

1935
Etching and engraving
8⅞ x 12″ (226 x 305 mm)
Sasowsky 159 IV/IV
Anonymous gift
61-186-30

The crowds on the beach at Coney Island, where "a million near naked bodies could be seen at once," was for Marsh "a phenomenon unparalleled in history," providing the subject he preferred most. In the early 1920s, as Marsh recalled, he was sent by his employer to Coney Island to make a drawing and continued "going out there every summer since, sometimes three or four days a week. In the winter I find the same themes on the streets, or in theaters, but Coney Island is best. . . . I like to go to Coney Island because of the sea, the open air, and the crowds—crowds of people in all directions, in all positions, without clothing, moving—like the great compositions of Michelangelo and Rubens. I failed to find anything like it in Europe."* A painting of this same subject from the same year is in the William Benton Museum of Art (University of Connecticut, Storrs).

*Quoted in Lloyd Goodrich, *Reginald Marsh* (New York, 1972), p. 38.

95
Eltinge Follies

1940
Engraving
12 x 9⅞″ (305 x 250 mm)
Sasowsky 211 VI/VII
Gift of Reginald Marsh
41-94-20

With his concentration on engraving in the 1940s, Marsh's line work became more deliberate and elegant. Effects of illumination and tone were often abandoned to allow the sculptural forms of his figures to attain their fullest expression.

1940
R.M.

Raphael Soyer

Born Borisoglebsk, Russia 1899

While paintings of women, especially the nude, have been the principal theme of Raphael Soyer's career, subjects of New York—shopgirls, street scenes, the Lower East Side—also have occupied his interest, particularly during the 1930s and 1940s. During his childhood in Russia, he spent much time drawing, encouraged by his parents. He had no formal training, however, until his family settled in New York, where he took various classes at the Cooper Union (1914–17), the National Academy of Design (1918–22), and the Art Students' League (1920–21, 1923, and 1926). Soyer first exhibited his paintings in 1926, and participated in the exhibitions of the Whitney Studio Club in 1927–28, but it was not until 1929, with the critical and financial success of his first one-man exhibition, that he was able to devote full time to his art. He exhibited regularly in the 1930s and, despite the ascendancy of the abstract movement in the 1950s and 1960s, he maintained a loyal following. Soyer found inspiration for his carefully observed paintings within his own environment—in familiar streets and among his family and friends—as well as in the canvases he has regularly studied in museums and galleries in America and Europe. He has expressed admiration for the Philadelphia artist Thomas Eakins as well as Rembrandt, Corot, Degas, and Pascin. Soyer first engaged in printmaking about 1916, when he bought a small etching press, but he executed only a few works in this medium until the mid-1930s. His earliest lithographs, drawn on transfer paper, date from about 1920; in 1933, when he began to draw directly on the stone, he first achieved the wide range of tones and the luminosity associated with his finest works.

96
Self-Portrait

1933
Lithograph
13¼ x 9¾" (336 x 248 mm)
Cole 26
Purchased: Thomas Skelton Harrison Fund
41-53-64

Soyer's continual probing of his subjects has also been directed toward himself in the many introspective self-portraits he has executed on canvas and on paper throughout his career.

97
The Mission

1933
Lithograph
12 3/16 x 17 5/8″ (310 x 448 mm)
Cole 27
Purchased: Lola Downin Peck Fund from the Carl and Laura Zigrosser Collection
74-24-215

Widely exhibited and reproduced during the Depression, this sympathetic lithograph of hopeless men being fed at a Bowery mission served as a reminder of the poverty rampant in America at the time.

RAPHAEL
SOYER

98
Toward the Light

1934–35
Lithograph
15 5/16 x 12 9/16" (389 x 319 mm)
Cole 35
Purchased: Thomas Skelton Harrison Fund
41-53-63

Light defines this figure of a nude—the artist's most favored subject—not only in the broadly illuminated areas toward the window but also in the darker shadows, where Soyer scratched away the crayon from the stone to extend the luminosity throughout the composition.

99
Bowery Nocturne

1933
Lithograph with black crayon
12 3/4 x 17 3/4" (324 x 451 mm)
Cole 28, unique trial proof
Anonymous gift
61-186-48

Masterful characterization emphasizes the individuality of each of the figures in this *Bowery Nocturne,* one of many paintings, drawings, and prints that Soyer did in the 1930s of the homeless and hungry on Fourteenth Street and the Bowery. This work's soft, atmospheric feeling, typical of Soyer's lithographs, was achieved through the subtle combination of textured grays. Soyer must not have been completely satisfied with this impression, however, for on this trial proof he darkened and defined the central figure by adding crayon lines on his back and collar.

Isabel Bishop

Born Cincinnati 1902

For over fifty years, Isabel Bishop has documented the people of New York, especially the denizens of Union Square and Fourteenth Street, where her studios have been located. In her paintings, drawings, and prints she has captured those who hurry down the street on their way to work, those who lounge in the park during their lunch hour, as well as those who loiter there throughout the day. After briefly studying art in Detroit, Bishop came to New York in 1918 and, intending to become a commercial artist, enrolled at the New York School of Applied Design for Women. Within two years she had abandoned this plan and was studying painting at the Art Students' League with Kenneth Hayes Miller and for a short time with Guy Pène du Bois. From Miller Bishop learned the value of fine draftsmanship, focusing on the figure as the principal element of design, and gained a respect for Renaissance art, which was reinforced when she, Reginald Marsh (q.v.), and Miller traveled together in Europe in 1931.* Miller also encouraged her choice of subjects from everyday life in the city. In 1936, Bishop began to teach at the Art Students' League and that same year she gained national attention when her painting *Two Girls* (1935) was purchased by the Metropolitan Museum of Art. Bishop first began to make etchings in the mid-1920s, generally depicting only one or two casually posed figures in her prints, which often serve as studies for her paintings.

* *See* Lawrence Alloway, "Isabel Bishop, the Grand Manner and the Working Girl," *Art in America,* vol. 63, no. 5 (September–October 1975), pp. 61–62.

100

Noon Hour

1935
Etching
6⅞ x 4¾″ (175 x 121 mm)
Staunton B. Peck Bequest
50-103-244

In this work Bishop portrayed two women on their lunch hour with an economy of line that deftly defines their form and gives substance to their figures. Bishop relies on her etchings as well as her many drawings as inspiration for the figures and groups in her larger compositions in oil. A later painting of the same subject, dated 1939, is in the Museum of Fine Arts, Springfield, Massachusetts.

101

Encounter

1939
Etching
8¼ x 5½″ (210 x 139 mm)
Gift of the Philadelphia Water Color Club
41-99-112

Here Bishop used a sketchlike line to concentrate on tone and illumination without, however, losing the solidity of her figures. A painting of *Encounter* from 1940 is in the Saint Louis Art Museum.

Yasuo Kuniyoshi

Okayama, Japan 1889*–1953 New York

Yasuo Kuniyoshi was trained in weaving and dyeing at a technical school in Japan before arriving in America in 1906. He studied at the Los Angeles School of Art and Design (1907–10), and then moved to New York in 1910, where he attended classes at various art schools—the National Academy of Design, the Henri School of Art, the Independent School of Art, and the Art Students' League. He first visited Europe in 1925, and on a second trip in 1928 worked with Jules Pascin, whose paintings of women in pensive, sensuous poses would influence his own work in the succeeding years. During his 1928 trip to Paris, Kuniyoshi concentrated on lithography, achieving a sense of color and atmosphere through working directly on the lithographic stone that he had not been able to capture in his earlier lithographs done on zinc plates. In 1933, Kuniyoshi began his twenty-year teaching career at the Art Students' League, and in 1936 he joined the graphics division of the Work Projects Administration (WPA). Throughout the 1930s and 1940s, he was very active in artists' organizations, and became the first president of Artists Equity in 1947. His retrospective exhibition at the Whitney Museum of American Art in New York in 1948 was the first given by that institution to a living artist.

* Recent evidence has suggested that Kuniyoshi was born in 1889, not 1893 as had been thought. *See* Austin, University of Texas, University Art Museum, *Yasuo Kuniyoshi,* 1889–1953*: A Retrospective Exhibition* (February 9–March 23, 1975), pp. 59–60.

102
Café No. 2
1936
Lithograph
12½ x 9¹³⁄₁₆" (318 x 250 mm)
Davis 67
Purchased: Lola Downin Peck Fund from the Carl and Laura Zigrosser Collection
74-24-136

Kuniyoshi is known for his individualistic style and his interest in the artistic process itself rather than the concern for realistic depiction expressed by many of his contemporaries. In this lithograph of a stylish woman at a café, the creative hand of the artist is clearly evident. Using a stylus to pick out white areas from his drawing on the stone, Kuniyoshi rapidly added the swirls in the fur and hair that give vigor to the composition and suggest the quickness of execution. A painting of the same subject, dated 1937, is in the Whitney Museum of American Art, New York.

Milton Avery

Altmar, New York 1893–1965
New York

The prints of Milton Avery were conceived quite independent of his colorful, energetic paintings of landscapes, seascapes, portraits, and nudes, although his thirty drypoints, most executed between 1933 and 1948, share many of the same subjects and the same vitality of execution. Little is known about Avery's art education, but he did study painting for a brief period in 1923 at the Connecticut League of Art Students in Hartford, where his family had moved in 1905. He went to New York in 1925 and began to exhibit there in 1928. By the early 1930s he was exhibiting his paintings regularly as his reputation grew; in 1960 a major retrospective exhibition of his work was held at the Whitney Museum of American Art in New York. Avery also executed twenty-one woodcuts from 1952 to 1955—mostly simple, whimsically depicted animals—and more than two hundred monotypes, begun after 1950.

103
Sally with Beret

1939
Drypoint
$7\frac{15}{16}$ x $6\frac{3}{8}$" (202 x 162 mm)
Gift of Harvey S. Shipley Miller
1981-53-1

Avery's stark portrait of his wife smoking a cigarette (barely visible on her right) anticipated the focus of a future generation of American printmakers which would turn from depiction of the American scene toward an expression of personal creativity. The rapid execution of the drypoint line and the distortions of the features emphasize more the personality of the sitter than the realistic details and structure of a portrait.

Robert Riggs

Decatur, Illinois 1896–1970
Philadelphia

Robert Riggs is known for his lithographs of prizefighting, circuses, and hospitals, filled with anecdotal detail and drawn from firsthand observation. The son of a printer,* Riggs grew up in Decatur, Illinois, where he studied art at the Decatur College and Industrial School from 1911 to 1913. He then attended the Art Students' League in New York on a scholarship in 1915–16. After service in Europe during World War I, he enrolled at the Académie Julian in Paris. In 1919 Riggs settled in Philadelphia, where he was employed by an advertising firm. After a period of extensive travel in the mid-1920s, he returned to Philadelphia to work as a free-lance illustrator for such magazines as *The Saturday Evening Post, Life,* and *Fortune,* winning renown and many awards for his art. The first important exhibition of his graphics took place in New York in 1933, when ten of his prizefight lithographs were shown and favorably reviewed by critics who compared both his subject and interpretation to those of George Bellows (q.v.) and Thomas Eakins.† Riggs executed at least eighty-two lithographs, most during the 1930s, including several series executed as promotional pieces for large corporations. Riggs taught in the illustration department of the Philadelphia Museum College of Art from 1961 to 1963.

* Dr. Ben Bassham, associate professor of art history, Kent State University, Kent, Ohio, has provided much of the present information from his research toward a catalogue raisonné of Riggs.

† *See* reviews from the *New York Times, New York Herald-Tribune,* and Henry McBride of the *New York Sun,* quoted in "A New Master," *The Art Digest,* vol. 7, no. 13 (April 1, 1933), p. 21.

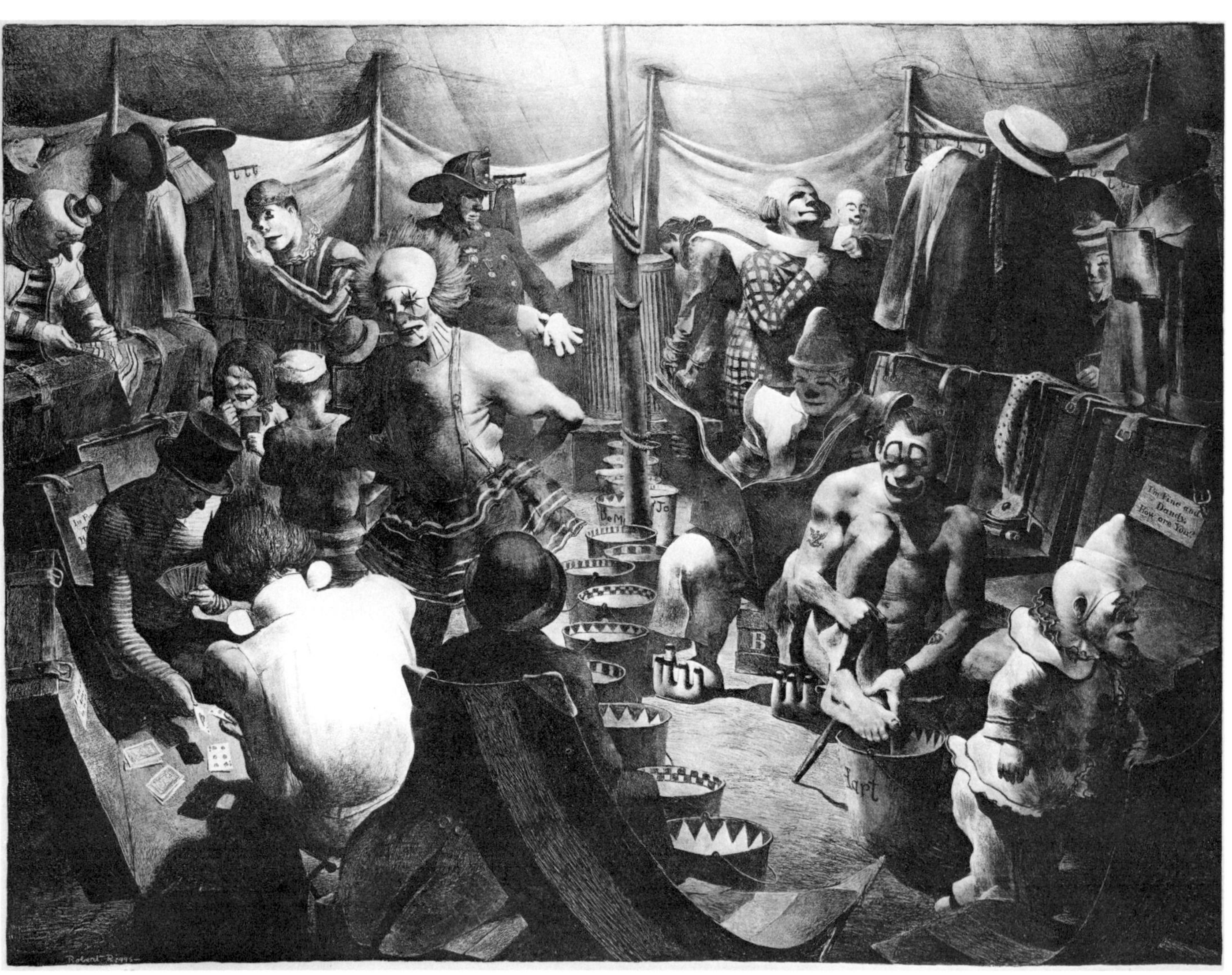

104
Clown Alley

c. 1937
Lithograph
$14^{3}/_{8}$ x $19^{1}/_{16}$" (365 x 484 mm)
Gift of the Philadelphia Water Color Club
41-99-74

The three-ring circus provided a wealth of material for Riggs, who not only captured the performances but also documented the anecdotal, behind-the-scenes activity of the performers. This lithograph, like many of his works, was executed using a subtractive method not unlike the commercial scratchboard technique. The stone was covered completely with grease crayon which was scratched away with a single-edge razor to create the composition.

105
Psychopathic Ward

c. 1939
Lithograph
$14^{5}/_{16}$ x $18^{7}/_{8}$" (363 x 479 mm)
Gift of R. Sturgis Ingersoll
46-80-8

Like Bellows's *Dance in a Madhouse* (no. 33), Riggs's *Psychopathic Ward* was based on real life; he composed it from studies he executed at the Philadelphia State Hospital for the Mentally Ill in Byberry.

106
Club Fighter

c. 1939
Lithograph
14 x 18⅛″ (356 x 460 mm)
Purchased: Thomas Skelton Harrison Fund
44-53-300

Prizefighting and neighborhood gyms intrigued Riggs, who, like Bellows (*see* no. 34), depicted both famous matches as well as now-forgotten club fighters. Riggs typically focused on the characterization of his protagonists rather than on the action of the fight. The broken nose and square features, the powerful tension of the muscular body, and the aggressive stance of this figure suggest the prototypical image of the prizefighter.

John Steuart Curry

Dunavant, Kansas 1897–1946
Madison, Wisconsin

Of the three Regionalists—Grant Wood, Thomas Hart Benton (qq.v.), and John Steuart Curry—Curry was the first to be recognized for his paintings focusing on the American Midwest and idealizing the values inherent in rural life. Curry had studied at the Kansas City Art Institute for only a month in 1916 when he decided to attend the Art Institute of Chicago, where he remained until 1918. Living in New Jersey, New York, and then Westport, Connecticut, he successfully pursued the career of an illustrator from 1921 to 1926, particularly being called upon to illustrate Western stories for *The Saturday Evening Post* and other magazines. In 1926 Curry went to Paris, studying for a year in the studio of a little-known Russian painter Basil Schoukhaeff. One of the paintings he completed on his return from Europe, *Baptism in Kansas* (Whitney Museum of American Art, New York), brought him his first public recognition when it was exhibited at the Corcoran Gallery of Art in Washington, D.C., in 1928. On a visit to his parents' farm the next year, Curry sketched the Kansas scenery that he was to draw upon for his subjects in the future. By 1930, with his first one-man exhibition at the Whitney Studio Club in New York, he had achieved national renown and his works were being acquired by museums. Curry taught at the Art Students' League in New York from 1932 to 1936 and at the Cooper Union from 1932 to 1934; in 1936 he moved West, accepting the post of artist-in-residence at the University of Wisconsin. Like many American artists during the 1930s, Curry painted murals for public buildings under federal programs, including several in Connecticut and Washington, D.C., and a cycle for the Kansas State Capitol in Topeka (1938–40), the latter financed by public subscription. Curry began to make lithographs in 1927 at the Art Students' League, and between 1934 and 1945 ten of his lithographs were published by the Associated American Artists. This gallery encouraged the Regionalists and other artists to work in graphics. Using revolutionary marketing techniques, the organization circulated these prints through department stores, mail orders, and advertisements. The unusually low prices and large editions successfully popularized lithography and at the same time provided both a wider access and more democratic approach to art, and increased financial return for the artists.

107
Danbury Fair

1930
Lithograph
13 x 9¾″ (330 x 248 mm)
Cole 8, Czestochowski C-8
Gift of Frederic Newlin Price
50-111-2

Curry was drawn to circuses and fairgrounds, such as the fair held annually in Danbury, Connecticut, not too far from his home in Westport. In 1932, Curry accompanied the spring tour through New England of the famed Ringling Brothers Barnum and Bailey Circus, which inspired a number of circus paintings and lithographs.

108
Mississippi Noah

1934
Lithograph
9⅞ x 13¾" (251 x 349 mm)
Cole 24, Czestochowski C-25
Gift of Frederic Newlin Price
50-111-5

Curry was intrigued with nature's destructive phenomena—floods, tornadoes, storms—as well as with nature's beauty. This lithograph of a Mississippi family taking refuge from the rising flood waters on the roof of their house is derived from sketches Curry made of a flood he had witnessed in Kansas in 1929. A painting of this subject, *The Mississippi,* of 1935, is in the Saint Louis Art Museum.

109
John Brown

1939
Lithograph
14¹¹⁄₁₆ x 10⅞" (373 x 277 mm)
Cole 34, Czestochowski C-35
Anonymous gift
61-186-13

This figure of the fiery abolitionist John Brown, who in 1859 made a daring raid on the federal arsenal at Harpers Ferry, Virginia, in an attempt to incite a slave uprising, was conceived for Curry's murals at the Kansas State Capitol. The cycle included three separate murals: *The Tragic Prelude,* showing John Brown and the beginning of the Civil War; *Kansas Pastoral,* idealizing the state and its citizens; and scenes of pioneer homesteaders in Kansas, which was never executed. A painting of John Brown, of 1939, similar to this lithograph, is in the Metropolitan Museum of Art, New York.

Thomas Hart Benton

Neosho, Missouri 1889–1975 Kansas City, Missouri

The most articulate of the Regionalists, Thomas Hart Benton explained the success of these champions of rural values in his book *An Artist in America:* "We symbolized aesthetically what the majority of Americans had in mind—America itself. Our success was a popular success. Even where some American citizens did not agree with the nature of our images . . . they understood them. What ideological battles we had were in American terms and were generally comprehensible to Americans as a whole. This was exactly what we wanted."* The son of a United States congressman, Benton spent much of his early life in Washington, D.C. He studied at the Art Institute of Chicago in 1907–8 and went to Paris in 1908, enrolling at the Académie Julian and also painting at the Académie Colarossi. He painted in styles ranging from academic realism to Pointillism and Cubism. When Benton returned to America in 1911, he worked as a commercial artist and continued painting, showing in New York in 1916 works in a Synchromist style influenced by his close friend Stanton MacDonald-Wright. While in the Navy during World War I, he began reading American history and drawing his observations of American life, past and present, which led him back to representation and marked the beginning of his series of mural-size paintings, *American Historical Epic,* based, however, on Renaissance models. In the mid-1920s, Benton started teaching at the Art Students' League in New York and at the same time began to travel in the rural areas of America, where he found subjects for his rhythmic and dramatic compositions. The 1930s brought him a number of large mural commissions: for the New School for Social Research (1930) and the Whitney Museum of American Art in New York (1932), for the State of Indiana's exhibit at the Chicago World's Fair (1933), and for the Missouri State Capitol in Jefferson City (1935–36). His friendship with John Steuart Curry (q.v.), whom he met in 1931, and Grant Wood (q.v.), whom he met in 1934, established the triumvirate of American Regionalism. In 1935 Benton left New York permanently, accepting a position as head of the painting department at the Kansas City Art Institute. He continued to exhibit frequently in New York, having already established a close relationship with the Associated American Artists, who circulated about fifty of his more than ninety lithographs.

* Thomas Hart Benton, *An Artist in America,* rev. ed. (New York, 1951), p. 315.

110
Going West

1934
Lithograph
12 3/16 x 23 5/16" (310 x 592 mm)
Anonymous gift
52-80-28

Benton described this lithograph as an "imaginative conception of a fast moving train. Steam powerd [*sic*] railroad trains were fascinating all my life. The Diesels have never had the same interest for me."*

* Creekmore Fath, comp. and ed., *The Lithographs of Thomas Hart Benton* (Austin, Tex., 1969), p. 32.

111
Frankie and Johnnie

1936
Lithograph
16 9/16 x 22 1/8" (420 x 562 mm)
Purchased: Thomas Skelton Harrison Fund
1979-96-7

Benton's celebration of the American scene included its folklore and folk songs. This lithograph reproduces a section of Benton's murals at the Missouri State Capitol. It recounts an incident that according to legend occurred in a Saint Louis bar, when Frankie discovered that her man Johnnie had been unfaithful:

Frankie went back to the bar-room,
As she rang the bar-room bell,
She said, 'Clear out all you people,
I'm gonna blow this man to hell.
  He was my man,
  But he done me wrong.'
. . . .
First time she shot him he staggered,
Second time she shot him he fell,
Third time she shot him, Oh, Lordy,
There was a new man's face in hell.
  She shot her man,
  'Cause he done her wrong.*

* Quoted in Creekmore Fath, comp. and ed., *The Lithographs of Thomas Hart Benton* (Austin, Tex., 1969), p. 42.

112
Cradling Wheat

1939
Lithograph
9 9/16 x 12″ (243 x 305 mm)
Purchased: Lola Downin Peck Fund from the Carl and Laura Zigrosser Collection
73-12-413

Benton looked to the old masters for inspiration for many of his paintings, both for subject—including a number of mythological works—and composition. Robert F. Chirico has suggested that this scene of farmers cutting wheat, cradling it in bunches, and then tying it into sheaves has its antecedent in the famous Pieter Brueghel painting of 1565, *The Harvesters,* in the Metropolitan Museum of Art, New York.* Benton's painting of *Cradling Wheat,* from 1938, is in the Saint Louis Art Museum.

* "Thomas Hart Benton and Pieter Bruegel," *Arts Magazine,* vol. 54, no. 1 (September 1979), pp. 148–49.

113
Fertility

1939
Lithograph
8 15/16 x 11 7/8″ (227 x 302 mm)
Czestochowski W-12
Gift of Dr. Matthew T. Moore
1978-23-6

It is not surprising that this simple house, silo, barn, and cornfield interested a man who said "my very best ideas of art had come to me while milking a cow in Iowa."* Wood's lithographs have a fine coloristic sense achieved through the use of dark and light contrasts and the manipulation of a wide range of gray tones.

* Quoted in Davenport, Iowa, Davenport Municipal Art Gallery, *This Is Grant Wood Country* (Davenport, 1977), p. 48.

Grant Wood

Anamosa, Iowa 1891–1942 Iowa City

Grant Wood became a leading figure in American art when the exhibition in 1930 of his painting *American Gothic* (Art Institute of Chicago) met with immediate critical acclaim. Focusing on rural subjects painted with precision and order, his work gave the impression of a harmony and stability in American life that contrasted with the anxiety and poverty of the Depression. Unlike his fellow Regionalists John Steuart Curry and Thomas Hart Benton (qq.v.), Wood never moved East, considering the big cities dominated by European culture, as he explained in his essay *Revolt Against the City* (Iowa City, 1935). He did, however, travel abroad frequently during the 1920s, observing "I had to go to France to appreciate Iowa. That was the best way to get perspective."* Wood studied at the Minneapolis School of Design, Handicraft, and Normal Art in 1910 and 1911 and took classes at the Art Institute of Chicago from 1913 through 1916, working at the same time as a jewelry designer. After serving in the army in 1917–18, Wood became a high school art teacher in Cedar Rapids, Iowa, exhibiting his Impressionist-style paintings locally over the next years. He first traveled abroad in 1920, and in 1923–24 was again in Europe, studying at the Académie Julian in Paris and painting in Italy and in the French provinces; in the summer of 1926 he returned to Paris. By this time he was receiving various illustration and mural commissions in Cedar Rapids, and work on one of them, a large stained-glass window, took Wood to Munich in 1928; there he was inspired by the paintings of the Flemish and German masters. On his return to Cedar Rapids he began to paint his surroundings with a geometrical organization, idealized simplicity, and precise style characteristic of his mature works. During the 1930s Wood designed murals and taught and lectured extensively. He helped to establish the Stone City Colony and Art School, where he taught during the summers of 1932 and 1933, and became associate professor of fine arts at the University of Iowa in 1934. In 1937, Grant Wood made the first of his nineteen lithographs, all but one of which were published by the Associated American Artists.

* Quoted in Davenport, Iowa, Davenport Municipal Art Gallery, *This Is Grant Wood Country* (Davenport, 1977), p. 16.

114
Tree Planting

1937
Lithograph
8 3/8 x 10 13/16″ (213 x 275 mm)
Czestochowski W-3
Purchased: Thomas Skelton Harrison Fund
41-53-73

In a style characteristic of Wood, the deliberate groupings and solid forms give a sense of importance and grandeur to this simple scene of schoolchildren looking to the future of their land as they join together in bringing trees and shade to the Great Plains.

115
Honorary Degree

1937
Lithograph
11 7/8 x 6 15/16″ (301 x 176 mm)
Czestochowski W-7
Purchased: Lola Downin Peck Fund from the Carl and Laura Zigrosser Collection
74-24-245

In 1936, Wood received an honorary degree from the University of Wisconsin in Madison, the first of a number of such distinctions that would be accorded him. In this lithograph which satirizes America's liberality with such honors, Wood used portraits of two fellow faculty members at the University of Iowa for the figures handing Wood his scroll and bestowing his hood, although he never received an honorary degree from this university.

Selected Bibliography

General

"American Drawings, Watercolors, and Prints." *The Metropolitan Museum of Art Bulletin,* vol. 37, no. 4 (Spring 1980), pp. 1–52.

Beall, Karen F. et al., comps. *American Prints in the Library of Congress: A Catalog of the Collection.* Baltimore, 1970.

Boston, Museum of Fine Arts. *American Prints 1813–1913.* April 12–June 15, 1975.

Boston, Museum of Fine Arts. *Art & Commerce: American Prints of the Nineteenth Century.* Charlottesville, Va., 1978.

Brussels, Bibliothèque Royale Albert Ier. *American Prints 1913–1963.* March 27–May 8, 1976. Catalogue by Riva Castelman.

Castelman, Riva. *Prints of the Twentieth Century: A History.* New York, 1976.

Johnson, Una E. *American Prints and Printmakers: A Chronicle of Over 400 Artists and Their Prints from 1900 to the Present.* Garden City, N.Y., 1980.

London, British Museum. *American Prints 1879–1979.* 1980. Catalogue by Frances Carey and Antony Griffiths.

New York, Hirschl & Adler Galleries. *America in Print 1796–1941.* April 2–25, 1981.

New York, Whitney Museum of American Art. *Turn-of-the-Century America: Paintings, Graphics, Photographs, 1890–1910.* June 30–October 2, 1977. Catalogue by Patricia Hills.

Smithsonian Institution, Traveling Exhibition Service. *The Image of Urban Optimism.* 1977. Catalogue by Jane M. Farmer.

Weitenkampf, F. *American Graphic Art.* New York, 1912.

Zigrosser, Carl. *The Artist in America: Twenty-Four Close-Ups of Contemporary Printmakers.* New York, 1942.

Zigrosser, Carl. *Prints and Their Creators: A World History.* 2d rev. ed. New York, 1974.

Zigrosser, Carl. *A World of Art and Museums.* Philadelphia, 1975.

Milton Avery

Una E. Johnson. *Milton Avery: Prints and Drawings, 1930–1964.* New York, 1966.

Harry H. Lunn, Jr., comp. and ed. *Milton Avery: Prints 1933–1955.* Washington, D.C., 1973.

George Bellows

Thomas Beer and Emma S. Bellows, comps. *George W. Bellows: His Lithographs.* New York, 1927.

Charles H. Morgan. *George Bellows: Painter of America.* New York, 1965.

Lauris Mason and Joan Ludman. *The Lithographs of George Bellows: A Catalogue Raisonné.* Millwood, N.Y., 1977.

Thomas Hart Benton

Creekmore Fath, comp. and ed. *The Lithographs of Thomas Hart Benton.* Austin, Tex., 1969.

Matthew Baigell. *Thomas Hart Benton.* New York, 1973.

Memphis, Tenn., Brooks Memorial Art Gallery. *A Question of Regionalism: Lithographs by Thomas Hart Benton, John Steuart Curry, Grant Wood.* 1975. Catalogue by Joseph S. Czestochowski.

Isabel Bishop

Una E. Johnson and Jo Miller. *Isabel Bishop: Prints and Drawings, 1925–1964.* New York, 1964.

Karl Lunde. *Isabel Bishop.* New York, 1975.

Mary Cassatt

Frederick A. Sweet. *Miss Mary Cassatt: Impressionist from Pennsylvania.* Norman, Okla., 1966.

New York, The Museum of Graphic Art. *The Graphic Art of Mary Cassatt.* 1967–68. Catalogue by Adelyn D. Breeskin and Donald H. Karshan.

Adelyn Dohme Breeskin. *Mary Cassatt: A Catalogue Raisonné of the Graphic Work.* 2d rev. ed. Washington, D.C., 1979.

William Merritt Chase

Katharine Metcalf Roof. *The Life and Art of William Merritt Chase.* New York, 1917.

Southampton, N.Y., The Parrish Art Museum. *William Merritt Chase in the Company of Friends.* May 13–June 14, 1979. Catalogue by Ronald G. Pisano.

New York, The Metropolitan Museum of Art. *The Painterly Print: Monotypes from the Seventeenth to the Nineteenth Century,* pp. 148–53, nos. 48–50. October 16–December 7, 1980.

John Steuart Curry

Memphis, Tenn., Brooks Memorial Art Gallery. *A Question of Regionalism: Lithographs by Thomas Hart Benton, John Steuart Curry, Grant Wood.* 1975. Catalogue by Joseph S. Czestochowski.

Sylvan Cole, Jr., comp. and ed. *The Lithographs of John Steuart Curry: A Catalogue Raisonné.* New York, 1976.

Joseph S. Czestochowski. *John Steuart Curry and Grant Wood: A Portrait of Rural America.* Columbia, Mo., 1981.

Arthur B. Davies

Frederic Newlin Price, comp. *The Etchings & Lithographs of Arthur B. Davies.* New York, 1929.

New York, The Association of American Artists. *Arthur B. Davies: An Exhibition of a Collection of Etchings, Drypoints and Lithographs.* November 1–26, 1966.

Tucson, Tucson Art Center. *Arthur B. Davies: Paintings and Graphics.* March 4–April 1, 1967.

Brooks Wright. *The Artist and the Unicorn: The Lives of Arthur B. Davies* (1862–1928). New City, N.Y., 1978.

Stuart Davis

James Johnson Sweeney. *Stuart Davis.* New York, 1945.

E. C. Goossen. *Stuart Davis.* New York, 1959.

New York, The Brooklyn Museum. *Stuart Davis: Art and Art Theory.* January 21–March 19, 1978. Catalogue by John R. Lane.

New York, Whitney Museum of American Art. *Stuart Davis.* August 20–October 12, 1980. Catalogue by Patterson Sims.

Lyonel Feininger

Hans Hess. *Lyonel Feininger.* New York, 1954.

Leona E. Prasse. *Lyonel Feininger. A Definitive Catalogue of His Graphic Work: Etchings, Lithographs, Woodcuts.* Cleveland, 1972.

Marsden Hartley

Elizabeth McCausland. "The Lithographs of Marsden Hartley." *Artist's Proof,* no. 3 (Spring 1962), pp. 30–32.

Lawrence, The University of Kansas, Museum of Art. *Marsden Hartley: Lithographs and Related Works.* March 19–April 16, 1972.

New York, Whitney Museum of American Art. *Marsden Hartley.* March 4–May 25, 1980. Catalogue by Barbara Haskell.

Childe Hassam

Royal Cortissoz. *Catalogue of the Etchings and Dry-Points of Childe Hassam, N.A.* New York, 1925.

Adeline Adams. *Childe Hassam.* New York, 1938.

Fuller Griffith. *The Lithographs of Childe Hassam: A Catalog.* Washington, D.C., 1962.

New York, The Metropolitan Museum of Art. *Childe Hassam as Printmaker: A Selection of Various Media.* June 28–September 11, 1977. Catalogue by David W. Kiehl and Doreen Bolger Burke.

Edward Hopper

Philadelphia, Philadelphia Museum of Art. *The Complete Graphic Work of Edward Hopper.* October–November 1962.

New York, Whitney Museum of American Art. *Edward Hopper.* September 29–November 29, 1964. Catalogue by Lloyd Goodrich.

Gail Levin. *Edward Hopper: The Complete Prints.* New York, 1979.

Rockwell Kent

Rockwell Kent and Carl Zigrosser. *Rockwellkentiana.* New York, 1933.

Dan Burne Jones. *The Prints of Rockwell Kent: A Catalogue Raisonné.* Chicago, 1975.

David Traxel. *An American Saga: The Life and Times of Rockwell Kent.* New York, 1980.

Yasuo Kuniyoshi

Richard A. Davis. "The Graphic Work of Yasuo Kuniyoshi, 1893–1953." *Archives of American Art,* vol. 5, no. 3 (July 1965), pp. 1–19.

Austin, University of Texas, University Art Museum. *Yasuo Kuniyoshi, 1889–1953: A Retrospective Exhibition.* February 9–March 23, 1975.

Martin Lewis
New York, Kennedy Galleries. *Martin Lewis: The Graphic Work.* April 11–28, 1973.

New York, Kennedy Galleries. *Martin Lewis: Retrospective Exhibition.* April 11–28, 1973.

Storrs, University of Connecticut, The William Benton Museum of Art. *The Graphic Art of Martin Lewis.* October 14–November 19, 1978. Catalogue by Thomas P. Bruhn.

Louis Lozowick
Burlington, The University of Vermont, Robert Hull Fleming Museum. *Abstraction and Realism: 1923–1943. Paintings, Drawings, and Lithographs of Louis Lozowick.* March 14–April 18, 1971.

New York, Whitney Museum of American Art. *Louis Lozowick Lithographs.* November 21, 1972–January 1, 1973.

South Orange, N.J., Seton Hall University, Student Center Art Gallery. *Louis Lozowick, 1892–1973.* October 14–November 11, 1973. Catalogue by Barbara Wahl Kaufman.

Long Beach, Calif., Long Beach Museum of Art. *Louis Lozowick: American Precisionist Retrospective.* February 26–May 7, 1978.

John Marin
MacKinley Helms. *John Marin.* Boston, 1948.

Philadelphia, Philadelphia Museum of Art. *The Complete Etchings of John Marin.* January 17–March 17, 1969. Catalogue by Carl Zigrosser.

Sheldon Reich. *John Marin: A Stylistic Analysis and Catalogue Raisonné.* Vol. 1. Tucson, 1970.

Reginald Marsh
New York, Whitney Museum of American Art. *Reginald Marsh.* September 21–November 6, 1955.

Lloyd Goodrich. *Reginald Marsh.* New York, 1972.

Norman Sasowsky. *The Prints of Reginald Marsh: An Essay and Definitive Catalog of His Linoleum Cuts, Etchings, Engravings, and Lithographs.* New York, 1976.

B.J.O. Nordfeldt
El Paso, Tex., El Paso Museum of Art. *B.J.O. Nordfeldt in Retrospect.* February–April 1963.

Van Deren Coke. *Nordfeldt the Painter.* Albuquerque, 1972.

Joseph Pennell
Joseph Pennell. *The Adventures of an Illustrator.* Boston, 1925.

Louis A. Wuerth. *Catalogue of the Etchings of Joseph Pennell.* Boston, 1928.

Oberlin, Ohio, Oberlin College, Allen Memorial Art Museum. *The Stamp of Whistler,* pp. 185–89. October 2–November 6, 1977. Catalogue by Robert H. Getscher.

Middletown, Conn., Wesleyan University, Davison Art Center. *Prints and Drawings by Joseph Pennell,* 1860–1926. May 5–June 3, 1979. Catalogue by Jane F. Allinson.

Maurice Prendergast
Hedley Howell Rhys. *Maurice Prendergast* 1859–1924. Cambridge, Mass., 1960.

New York, Davis & Long Company. *The Monotypes of Maurice Prendergast: A Loan Exhibition.* April 4–28, 1979.

New York, The Metropolitan Museum of Art. *The Painterly Print: Monotypes from the Seventeenth to the Nineteenth Century,* pp. 156–67, nos. 52–58. October 16–December 7, 1980.

Robert Riggs
Henry C. Pitz. "The Resurgence of Robert Riggs." *American Artist,* vol. 30, no. 5 (May 1966), pp. 50–55, 81.

Philadelphia, Philadelphia Museum of Art. *Philadelphia: Three Centuries of American Art,* pp. 554–55, no. 470. April 11–October 10, 1976.

John Singer Sargent
William Howe Downes. *John S. Sargent, His Life and Work.* Boston, 1925.

Albert Belleroche. "The Lithographs of Sargent." *Print Collector's Quarterly,* vol. 13 (February 1926), pp. 30–45.

Richard Ormond. *John Singer Sargent: Paintings, Drawings, Watercolors.* New York, 1970.

Charles Sheeler
Iowa City, The University of Iowa. *The Quest of Charles Sheeler: 83 Works Honoring His 80th Year.* March 17–April 14, 1963.

Washington, D.C., Smithsonian Institution, National Collection of Fine Arts. *Charles Sheeler.* October 10–November 24, 1968. Catalogue by Martin Friedman, Barlett Hayes, and Charles Millard.

University Park, The Pennsylvania State University, Museum of Art. *Charles Sheeler: The Works on Paper.* February 10–March 24, 1974. Catalogue by John P. Driscoll.

John Sloan
Van Wyck Brooks. *John Sloan: A Painter's Life.* New York, 1955.

Carl Zigrosser. "The Graphic Work of John Sloan." *The Philadelphia Museum Bulletin,* vol. 51, no. 248 (Winter 1956), pp. 19–31.

Peter Morse. *John Sloan's Prints: A Catalogue Raisonné of the Etchings, Lithographs, and Posters.* New Haven, 1969.

Helen Farr Sloan, ed. *John Sloan: New York Etchings* (1905–1949). New York, 1978.

Raphael Soyer
New York, Whitney Museum of American Art. *Raphael Soyer.* October 25–December 3, 1967. Catalogue by Lloyd Goodrich.

Sylvan Cole, Jr., ed. *Raphael Soyer: Fifty Years of Printmaking,* 1917–1967. New York, 1967.

Niles Spencer
Holger Cahill. "Niles Spencer." *Magazine of Art,* vol. 45, no. 7 (November 1952), pp. 313–15.

Huntington, N.Y., Heckscher Museum. *The Precisionist Painters* 1916–1949: *Interpretations of a Mechanical Age.* July 7–August 20, 1978.

John Twachtman
Margery Austen Ryerson. "John H. Twachtman's Etchings." *Art in America,* vol. 8 (February 1920), pp. 92–96.

R. J. Wickenden. *The Art & Etchings of John Twachtman.* New York, 1921.

Cincinnati, The Cincinnati Art Museum. *A Retrospective Exhibition: John Henry Twachtman.* October 7–November 20, 1966.

Max Weber
Alfred Werner. *Max Weber.* New York, 1975.

Washington, D.C., Smithsonian Institution, National Collection of Fine Arts. *Max Weber: Prints and Color Variations.* July 11–October 5, 1980.

Daryl R. Rubenstein. *Max Weber: A Catalogue Raisonné of His Graphic Work.* Chicago, 1980.

James Abbott McNeill Whistler
Elizabeth Robins and Joseph Pennell. *The Life of James McNeill Whistler.* 2 vols. Philadelphia, 1908.

Edward G. Kennedy. *The Etched Work of Whistler. Illustrated by Reproductions in Collotype of the Different States of the Plates.* New York, 1910.

Thomas R. Way. *The Lithographs by Whistler. Illustrated by Reproductions in Photogravure and Lithography.* New York, 1914.

New York, Wildenstein. *From Realism to Symbolism: Whistler and His World.* March 4–April 3, 1971.

Oberlin, Ohio, Oberlin College, Allen Memorial Art Museum. *The Stamp of Whistler.* October 2–November 6, 1977. Catalogue by Robert H. Getscher.

Grant Wood
Memphis, Tenn., Brooks Memorial Art Gallery. *A Question of Regionalism: Lithographs by Thomas Hart Benton, John Steuart Curry, Grant Wood.* 1975. Catalogue by Joseph S. Czestochowski.

Davenport, Iowa, Davenport Municipal Art Gallery. *This Is Grant Wood Country.* Davenport, 1977. Catalogue by Joan Liffring-Zug.

Joseph S. Czestochowski. *John Steuart Curry and Grant Wood: A Portrait of Rural America.* Columbia, Mo., 1981.

William Zorach
New York, The Brooklyn Museum. *William Zorach: Paintings, Watercolors and Drawings,* 1911–1922. November 26, 1968–January 19, 1969. Catalogue by Donelson F. Hoopes.

Washington, D.C., Smithsonian Institution, National Collection of Fine Arts. *Modern American Woodcuts.* November 30, 1973–January 27, 1974.

Index of Artists